Sooo Big!
BABY QUILTS

Sooo Big! Baby Quilts

Landauer Publishing, www.landauerpub.com, is an imprint of Fox Chapel Publishing Company, Inc.

Copyright © 2021 by Fox Chapel Publishing Company, Inc., 903 Square Street, Mount Joy, PA 17552.

Project Team
Editorial Director: Kerry Bogert
Editor: Amy Deputato
Copy Editor/Indexer: Jean Bissell
Designer: Wendy Reynolds

ISBN 978-1-947163-71-3

Library of Congress Control Number: 2021935569

We are always looking for talented authors. To submit an idea, please send a brief inquiry to acquisitions@foxchapelpublishing.com.

Printed in Singapore
24 23 22 21   2 4 6 8 10 9 7 5 3 1

Sooo Big!
BABY QUILTS

33 Adorable Designs to Sew for Little Ones

Amelia Johanson, Editor

Quilts by Wendy Sheppard, Lynette Jensen, Suzanne McNeill,
Choly Knight, Mary M. Hogan, and other top quilters

Landauer Publishing

Contents

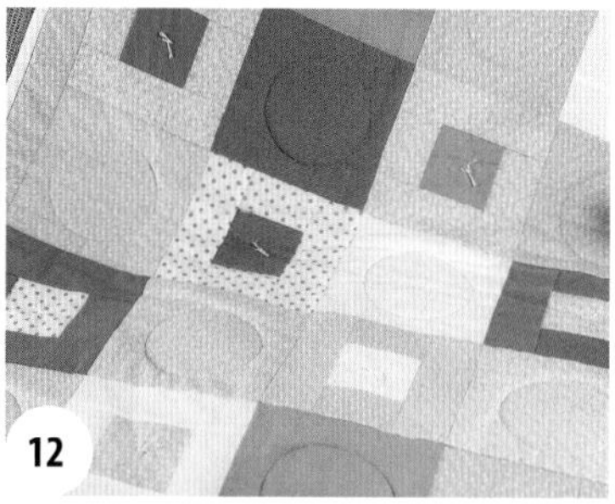

12

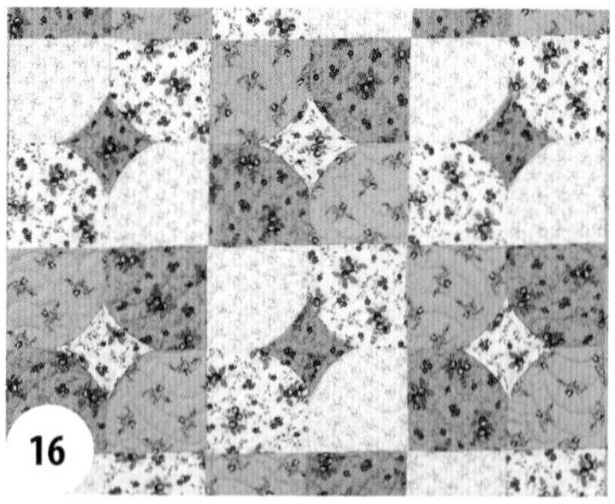

16

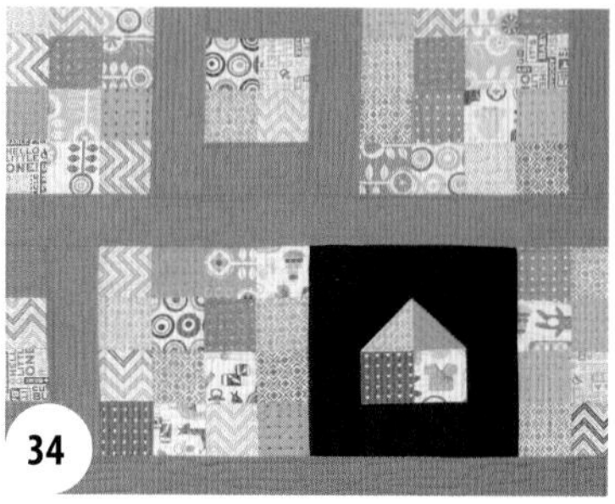

34

38

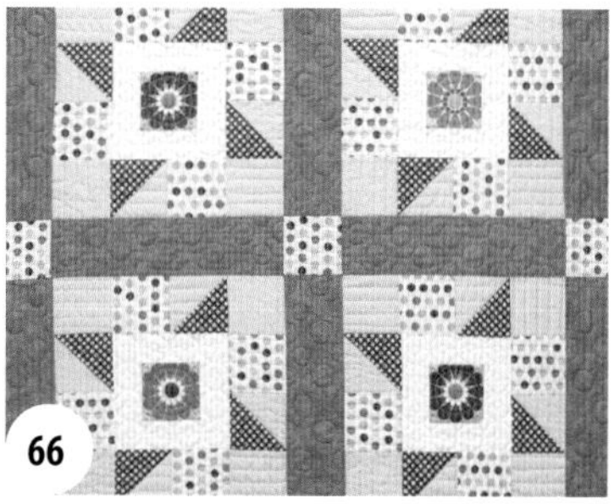

66

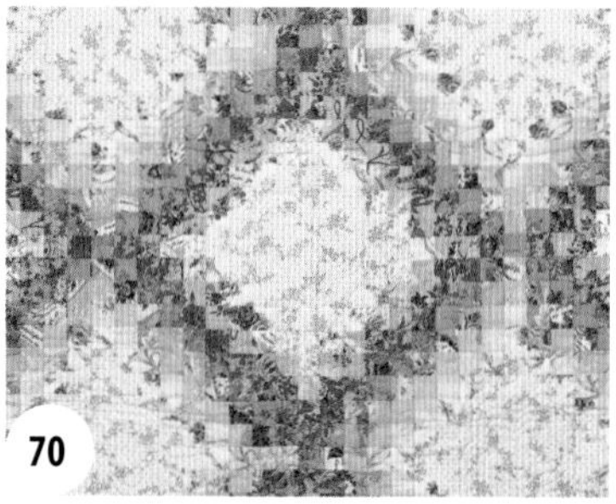

70

86

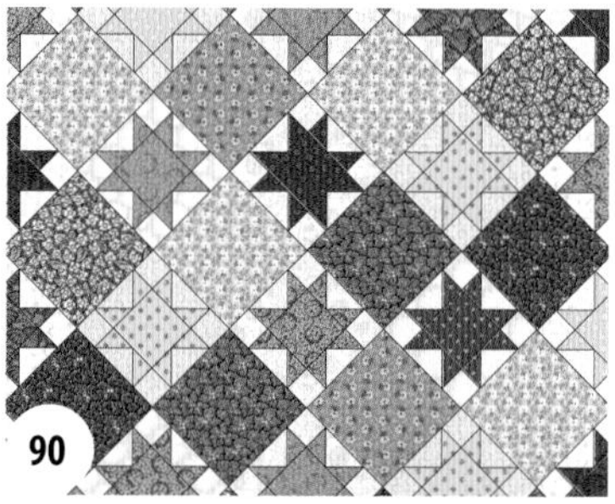

90

102

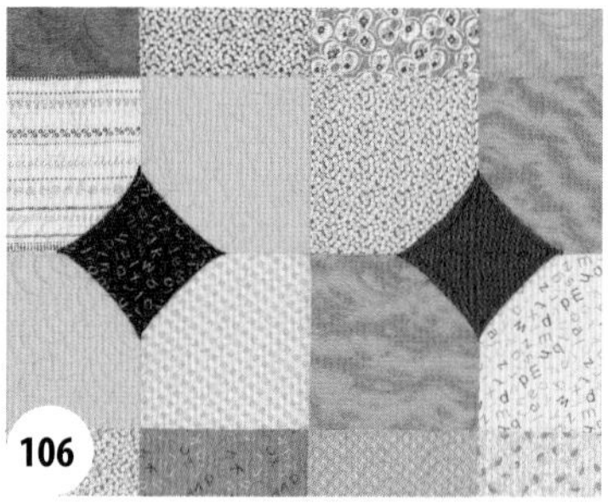

106

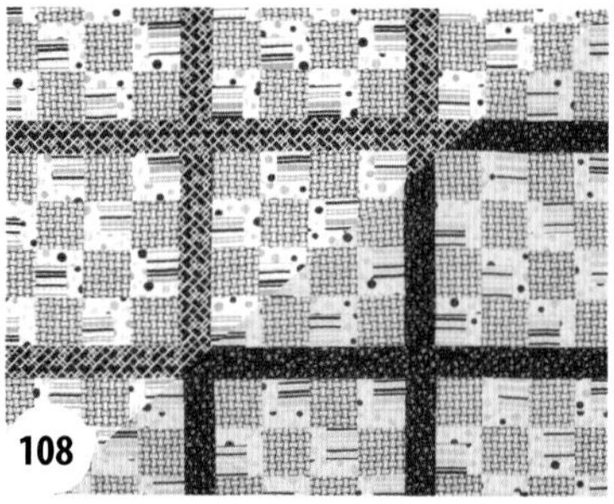

108

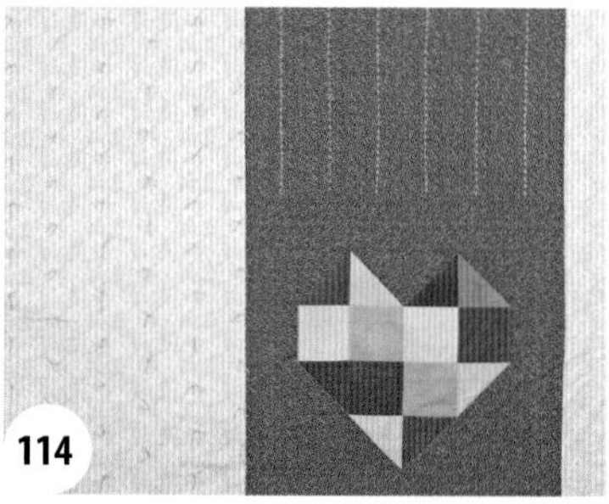

114

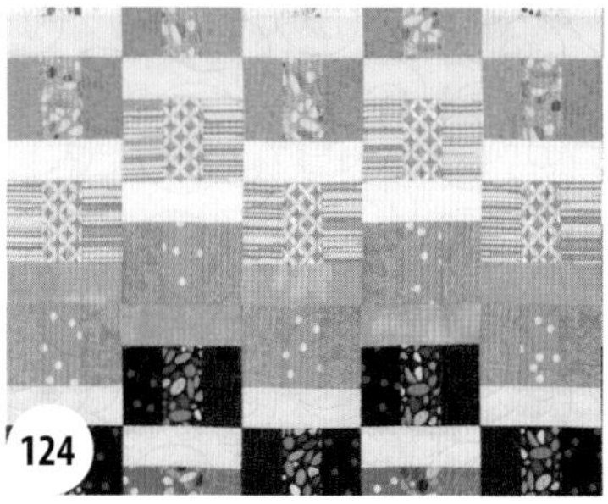

124

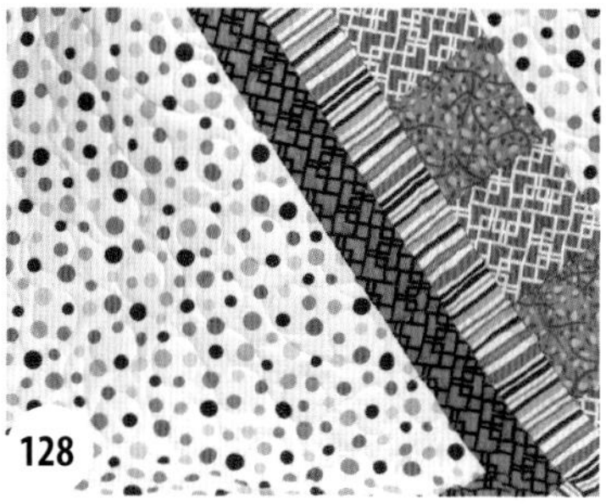

128

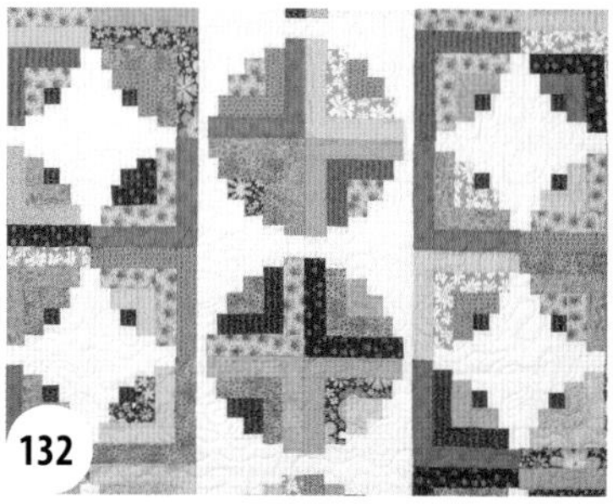

132

138

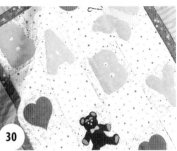

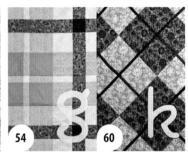

PART 2: FLOOR QUILTS

Introduction

There is such joy in making a baby quilt. Not only are the excitement and anticipation of welcoming a new little one infused into every stitch, but there are so few parameters to making it "right." You won't find a baby in the world who is going to worry about whether it's 66" x 35", 40" x 60", or any size in between. Baby quilts, unlike bed quilts, don't have to be sized properly to fit a mattress. In fact, in these modern times, baby quilts, which were traditionally called "crib" quilts, usually end up being tossed in the crib or port-a-bed when baby isn't in it.* Yet, there are so many other ways in which baby quilts are an all-important part of a layette. Anyone who has cared for a baby knows that not only can a baby quilt set the decor for the entire nursery, a well-loved baby quilt sees duty as a floor mat, a changing station, a nursing cover, an extra layer of protection to carry baby from house to car, and more. Other specialty designs can serve as wall hangings, like Spotted Stars on page 66, or as teaching tools, like Eye Spy on page 38—how fun it will be to fussy-cut all those novelty fabrics! Baby quilts in soft and subtle hues (Baby Cakes, page 122) have a soothing sensibility, while others with strong contrasting blocks (Echoes, page 132) serve to stimulate baby's development. Best of all, baby quilts are just as satisfying to make as larger quilts! You will still pore over selecting the perfect fabrics to go with just the right pattern, yet, because of the smaller size, you can perhaps indulge a bit in the materials or will even have time to make more than one.

You'll find thirty-three baby quilts in these pages, designed by some of our top quilting authors through the years. This is a beautiful collection that incorporates a variety of techniques and design styles while appealing to quilters of all skill levels. You're sure to find just the pattern you've been looking for.

Metric Conversion Chart		
TO CONVERT	**TO**	**MULTIPLY BY**
Inches	Centimeters	2.54
Centimeters	Inches	0.4
Feet	Centimeters	30.5
Centimeters	Feet	0.03
Yards	Meters	0.9
Meters	Yards	1.1

*The American Academy of Pediatrics (AAP) recommends keeping soft objects and loose bedding out of the baby's sleeping area for at least the first twelve months. This recommendation is based on data around infant sleep deaths and guidelines for reducing the risk of SIDS.

Helpful Tips

Basic Cutting Instructions

Tips for Accurate Cutting

Accurate cutting is easy when using a rotary cutter with a sharp blade, a cutting mat, and a transparent ruler. Begin by pressing your fabric and then follow these steps:

Folding

1. Fold the fabric with the selvage edges together. Smooth the fabric flat. If needed, fold again to make your fabric length shorter than the length of the ruler.

2. Align the fold with one of the guide lines on the mat. This is important to avoid getting a kink in your strip.

Cutting

1. Align the ruler with a guide line on the mat. Press down on the ruler to prevent it from shifting or have someone help hold the ruler. Hold the rotary cutter along the edge of the ruler and cut off the selvage edge.

2. Also using the guide line on the mat, cut the ends straight.

3. Cut strips for making the quilt top on the crosswise grain (from selvage to selvage) or on the grain (parallel to the selvage edge). If possible, cut strips for the borders on the grain to prevent wavy edges and make quilting easier.

Tip: When cutting strips, move the ruler, **not** the fabric.

Rotary Cutter Safety

A rotary cutter is a wonderful and useful tool. When not used correctly, the sharp blade can be dangerous. Follow these safety tips:

1. Never cut toward you.

2. Use a sharp blade. Pressing harder on a dull blade can cause the blade to jump the ruler and injure your fingers.

3. Always disengage the blade before the cutter leaves your hand, even if you intend to pick it up again immediately. A rotary cutter can get caught on fabric and fall to the floor, cutting feet, legs, or fingers on the way.

Pre-Cut Strips Tips

Pre-cut strips are cut on the crosswise grain and are prone to stretching. These tips will help reduce stretching and make your quilt lay flat for quilting.

1. If you are cutting yardage, cut on the grain.

2. When sewing crosswise grain strips together, take care not to stretch the strips. If you detect any puckering as you go, rip out the seam and sew it again.

3. Press. Do **not** iron. Carefully open fabric, with the seam to one side, and press without moving the iron. A back-and-forth ironing motion stretches the fabric.

4. Reduce the wiggle in your borders with this technique from garment making: First, accurately cut your borders to the exact measurements of the quilt top. Then, before sewing the border to the quilt, run a double row of stay stitches along the outside edge to maintain the original shape and prevent stretching. Pin the border to the quilt, taking care not to stretch the quilt top to make it fit. Pinning reduces slipping and stretching.

Matching Edges

1. Carefully line up the edges of your strips. Many times, if the underside is off a little, your seam will be off by ⅛". This does not sound like much until you have eight seams in a block, each off by ⅛". Now your finished block is a whole inch wrong!

2. Pin the pieces together to prevent them from shifting.

Seam Allowance

I cannot stress enough the importance of accurate seams. Many of the quilts in this book are measured for ¼" seams, but the seam allowance is indicated with each project.

Most sewing machine manufacturers offer a ¼" foot. Because ¼" seams are so common in quilting, a ¼" foot is a very worthwhile investment.

Sewing Bias Edges

Bias edges wiggle and stretch out of shape very easily. They are not recommended for beginners, but even a novice can accomplish bias edges if the following techniques are employed:

1. Stabilize the bias edge with one of these methods:

a) Press with spray starch.

b) Press freezer paper or removable iron-on stabilizer to the back of the fabric.

c) Sew a double row of stay stitches along the bias edge and ⅛" from the bias edge. This is a favorite technique of garment makers.

2. Pin, pin, pin! I know that many of us dislike pinning, but when working with bias edges, pinning makes the difference between intersections that match and those that do not.

Building Better Borders

Wiggly borders make a quilt very difficult to finish. However, wiggly borders can be avoided with the following steps:.

1. Cut the borders on the grain (parallel to the selvage edge).

2. Accurately cut your borders to the exact measurements of the quilt.

3. If your borders are piece-stripped from crosswise grain fabrics, press well with spray starch and sew a double row of stay stitches along the outside edge to maintain the original shape and prevent stretching.

4. Pin the border to the quilt, taking care not to stretch the quilt top to make it fit. Pinning reduces slipping and stretching.

Pressing

Proper pressing can make the difference between a quilt that wins a ribbon at the quilt show and one that does not.

As mentioned, you want to press, **not** iron. What does that mean? Moving the iron back and forth along the seam stretches the strip out of shape and creates errors that accumulate as the quilt is constructed. Following are instructions on how to press your seams:

1. Do not use steam with your iron. If you need a little water, spritz it on.

2. Place your fabric flat on the ironing board without opening the seam. Set the hot iron on the seam and count to three. Lift the iron and move to the next position along the seam. Repeat until the entire seam is pressed. This sets and sinks the threads into the fabric.

3. Carefully lift the top strip and fold it away from you so the seam is on one side. Usually the seam is pressed toward the darker fabric, but often the direction of the seam is determined by the piecing requirements.

4. Press the seam open with your fingers. Add a little water or spray starch if it wants to close again. Lift the iron and place it on the seam. Count to three. Lift the iron again and continue until the seam is pressed. Do not use the tip of the iron to push the seam open. So many people do this, and they wonder later why their blocks are not fitting together!

5. The most critical thing to know is that, for accuracy, every seam must be pressed before the next seam is sewn.

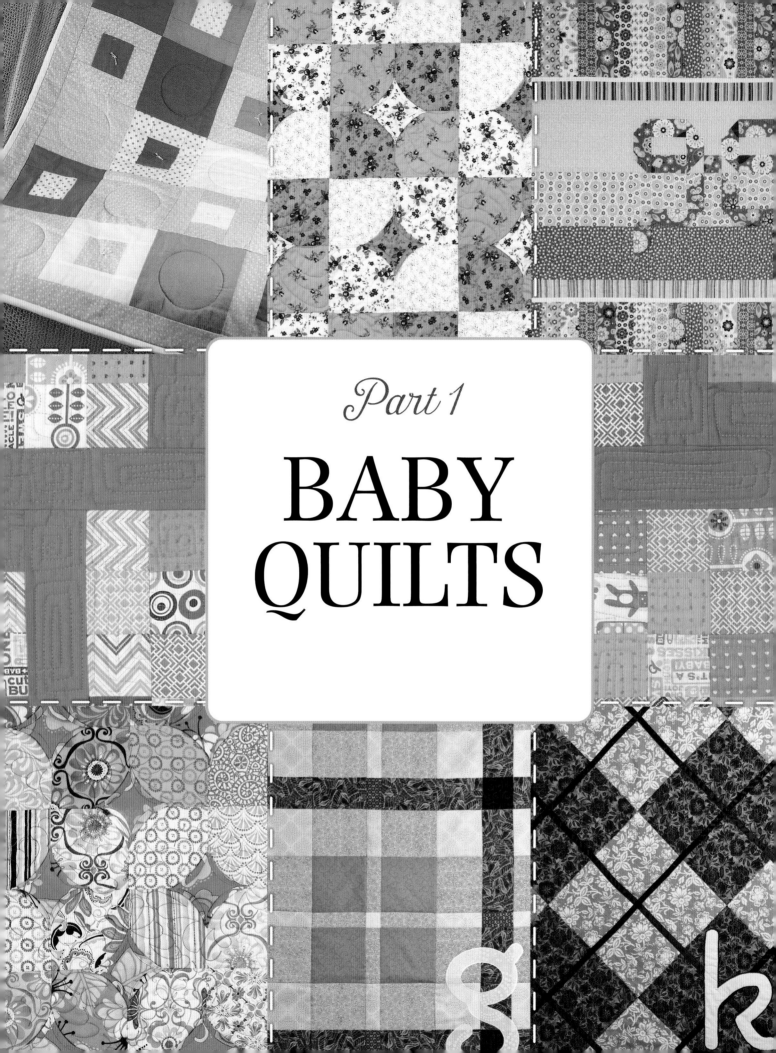

Part 1

BABY QUILTS

Dotty Quilt

By Rita Whitehorn
Finished size: 37" x 30" (86 x 71cm)

This little crib quilt is best suited to a baby from the age of one year upward, when he or she can move around more freely and kick off the cover if it becomes too warm. Its mixture of soft pastel blues, pinks, greens, and yellow will suit either a little boy or a little girl.

Materials

All fabrics used in the quilt top are 45"-wide, 100% cotton.
- **Print fabrics:** 9" of each of seven colors (I used pastel small flowery prints in yellow, green, pink, and blue, dotty prints in blue and white and pink and white, plus a white-on-white print.)
- **Plain fabrics:** 9" of each of four colors (I used pastels in shades of blue, pink, lilac, and green to match the prints.)
- ½ yard white-on-white print for binding
- ½ yard green flowery print for border
- 34" x 41" backing fabric
- 34" x 41" batting
- Template plastic and circle template on page 15
- Stranded embroidery cotton or perle

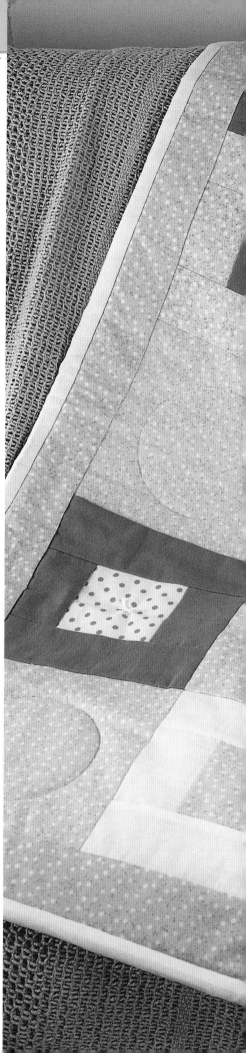

Quilt originally appeared in *Super-Quick Colorful Quilts*

Cutting

Follow the quilt assembly diagram on page 15 for the placement of the prints and plain fabrics. Alternatively, make your own color plan before you start.

1. From each of the print and plain fabrics (except the green print), cut one 3¼" x 3¼" square for the inner squares of the pieced blocks. You need a total of ten small squares.

2. From the print and plain fabrics (except the plain green), cut strips across the width of the fabric, 2¼" deep.

3. From the print and plain fabrics, cut ten squares 6¾" x 6¾" to alternate with the pieced blocks. You could have a different fabric for each square, but I chose not to use the stronger prints because they would be too dominant. I cut one each of plain pink, plain blue, and plain lilac; one each of pink print, white-on-white, and blue print; and two each of green print and yellow print.

4. From the green flowery print, cut four strips 2¼" deep across the width of fabric for the borders.

5. From the white-on-white print, cut four strips of fabric 2" deep across the width of the fabric for the binding.

Making the Blocks

1. Following the quilt assembly diagram for the correct matching of fabrics, place one fabric strip right sides together with one small square, aligning raw edges. Stitch with a ¼" seam allowance. Trim the strip level with the square (Fig. 1).

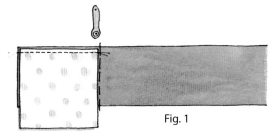

Fig. 1

2. Repeat to stitch the same strip to the bottom edge of the square and trim (Fig. 2a). Press the seams to the darker fabric (Fig. 2b).

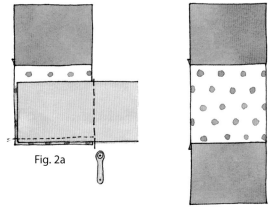

Fig. 2a

Fig. 2b

3. Repeat to stitch a strip to the right side of the block (Fig. 3a), then to the left (Fig. 3b). This completes the "square within a square" block.

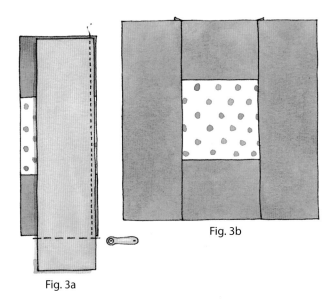

Fig. 3a

Fig. 3b

4. Still following the quilt assembly plan, stitch nine more blocks in the same way.

Quilt Top Assembly

1. Lay out the blocks, alternating with the larger plain squares in five rows of four squares.

2. Stitch the squares in each row together with a ¼" seam allowance, then pin and stitch the rows together, carefully matching seams.

3. Measure the pieced top through the center from top to bottom, then trim two of the border strips to this measurement. Stitch to each side of the top.

4. Measure the pieced top through the center from side to side, then trim two of the border strips to this measurement. Stitch to the top and bottom.

Finishing

1. Spread the backing right side down on a flat surface. Then smooth out the batting and the patchwork top, right side up, on the backing. Fasten together with safety pins or baste in a grid.

2. Using the template plastic, make a template from the circle shown at right. Use the template and marking pencil to mark circles in the center of each of the plain squares of the pieced top. Quilt around these circles by hand using large stitches.

3. To add ties to the quilt, lightly mark the center of each inner square of the pieced blocks. Thread a large needle with the embroidery cotton or perle and insert the needle ¼" to the right of the marked center point. Then bring needle out about ½" to the left of the entry point, leaving a "tail" of thread about 3" long. Put the needle back into the first hole and come back up into the same place as the first exit point. Cut the thread about 3" from this point. Tie a double knot but do not pull too tightly. Trim the thread to the length desired (Fig. 4).

Fig. 4

4. To bind the quilt, fold over ¼" of fabric to the wrong side on each of the binding strips and press.

5. Place the right side of the binding to the right side of the quilt top—raw edges to raw edges—and pin tack or baste. Then stitch with a ¼" seam allowance through all the layers. Trim off excess binding in line with the quilt top.

6. Fold over the binding to the wrong side of the quilt and slip stitch in place along the previously pressed-up edge with a thread that matches the binding fabric.

7. Repeat for the left side of the quilt. Add binding strips to the top and bottom in the same way, but turn in a small hem at each end of the strip before folding to the back and hemstitching.

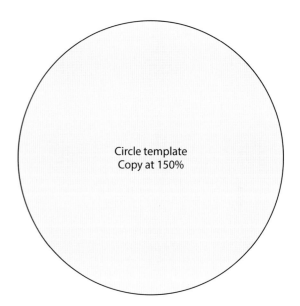

Circle template
Copy at 150%

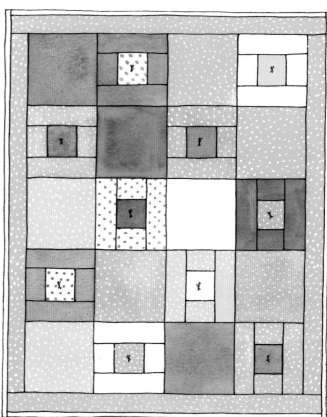

Quilt top assembly diagram

Easy Elegance

Designed by Suzanne McNeill, pieced by Edna Summers, quilted by Sue Needle
Finished size: 37" x 46" (94 x 117cm)

Pretty pastels capture the elegance of times past on a quilt that is assembled with a speed and ease that would amaze your grandmother.

Materials

- ½ yard blue large print for squares
- ⅓ yard white small print for squares
- ½ yard blue small print for squares and Border 1
- 1⅓ yards white large print for squares, Border 2, and binding
- 1⅔ yards backing fabric
- 45" x 54" batting
- AccuQuilt® GO! Me® fabric cutter and GO! die #55010 (Square 5"), or template plastic and template on page 150

Cutting

Use the fabric cutter or trace and cut out the following pieces:
- Eighteen white large print 5" squares
- Twelve white small print 5" squares
- Eighteen blue large print 5" squares
- Twelve blue small print 5" squares

For Border 1, cut:
- Two strips 1½" x 36½" for sides
- Two strips 1½" x 29½" for top and bottom

For Border 2, cut:
- Two strips 4½" x 38½" for sides
- Two strips 4½" x 37½" for top and bottom

Quilt originally appeared in *GO! Baby® Quilting*

Making the Blocks

Refer to the Ten-Minute Block instructions on page 18.

Block A
- Refer to diagram for placement of fabrics.
- Make six of Block A.

Block B
- Refer to diagram for placement of fabrics.
- Make six of Block B.

Blocks A and B
- Roll back the bias edge of each center square (page 19) to make a curved edge.
- Topstitch in place.

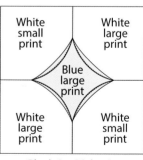

Block A—Make six

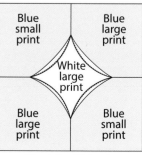

Block B—Make six

Quilt Top Assembly

1. Arrange four rows of three blocks each on a work surface.

2. Sew the rows together. Press.

Border 1

1. Cut two strips 1½"x 36½" for sides.

2. Cut two strips 1½" x 29½" for top and bottom.

3. Sew side borders to the quilt. Press.

4. Sew top and bottom borders to the quilt. Press.

Border 2

1. Cut two strips 4½"x 38½" for sides.

2. Cut two strips 4½" x 37½" for top and bottom.

3. Sew side borders to the quilt. Press.

4. Sew top and bottom borders to the quilt. Press.

Finishing

1. Quilt as desired.

2. Sew 2½" strips together end to end to equal 176".

3. Follow the binding instructions starting on page 58 or page 64.

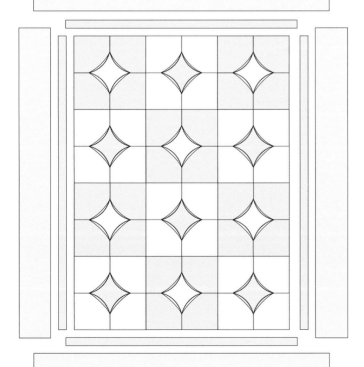

Quilt top assembly diagram

Basic Instructions for Ten-Minute Blocks

1. For each block, you will need four corner squares and one C center square.

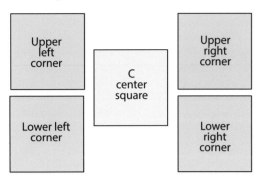

2. Fold the C center square in half with wrong sides together.

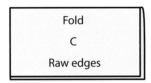

3. Align the raw edges of the C folded square with the bottom and left edges of the upper right corner square.

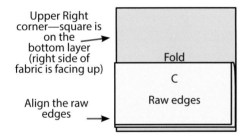

4. Sandwich the C folded square between the right sides of two corner squares so the right sides are touching C. There should be four layers of fabric along the bottom.

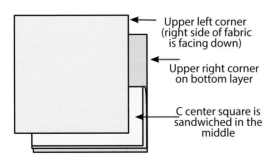

5. Align the four layers of fabric along the bottom.

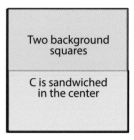

6. Sew a ¼" seam on the left-hand side.

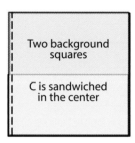

7. Open the layers so the corner squares meet with wrong sides together. Turn the piece to match the diagram.

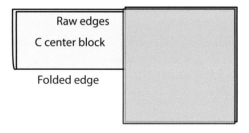

8. Place the lower right corner square under the C folded square (right side of fabric facing up). Align the top and left raw edges.

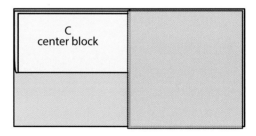

9. Place the lower left corner square on top (right side of fabric facing down). This layers the C folded square between the right sides of the corner squares. Align the left and top edges. Sew a ¼" seam on the left side.

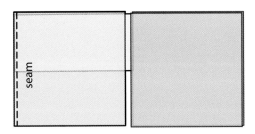

10. Open the corner squares with wrong sides together. Press.

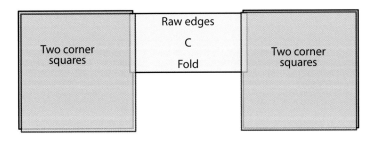

11. Pull the C center square apart.

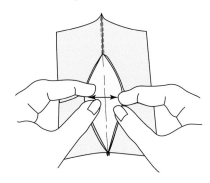

12. Flatten the seams with right sides together. (opening up the C center square so it makes a diamond)

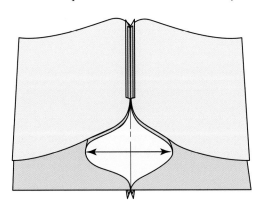

13. Pull the center shape until the shape is flat. Press.

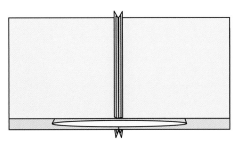

14. Pin the raw edges together making sure to line up the seams in the center.

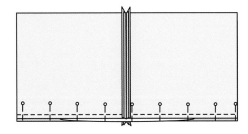

15. Sew a ¼" seam along the bottom edge.

16. Open the piece and pull the center shape until it is flat and the C center forms a layered diamond. Press.

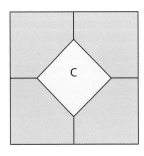

Cathedral Window

Create interesting curves in the center of each large block. This technique is simple and creates a wonderfully mysterious look.

  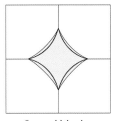

Gently pull the loose edge of each side of the center square toward the center of the block forming a curve.

Pin in place. Topstitch along the *inside* edges of each center block to hold the edges down flat.

Curved blocks in the center

Childhood Memories

By Wendy Sheppard

Finished quilt size: Approximately
36" x 45" (91 x 114cm)

Babies are gifts, and gifts need bows! This sweet quilt features a large bow block with wide accent borders.

Materials

Note: This project is a good way to use leftover jelly roll strips. Jelly roll strips need to be a minimum of 42" long for the featured quilt. If your jelly roll strips are shorter, you will need thirteen assorted print strips instead of twelve.
- Twelve 2½" x WOF assorted print strips
- One 2½" x WOF solid white strip
- Two yellow print fat quarters
- Two blue print fat quarters
- Two pink print fat quarters
- One brown print fat quarter
- Five 2½" x WOF strips for binding
- 42" x 50" backing fabric
- 42" x 50" batting

Jelly roll strip = 2½" x WOF
WOF = width of fabric
Sew with ¼" seam allowance unless otherwise noted.

Cutting

From nine assorted print strips, cut:
- Four 2½" x 10½" rectangles from each strip for a total of thirty-six rectangles

From three assorted print strips, cut:
- Three 2½" x 36½" sashing strips

From the white solid strip, cut:
- Two 1" x 36½" sashing strips

From one of each yellow, blue, and pink print fat quarters, cut:
- One 4½" x 6½" rectangle
- One 6½" x 14½" rectangle

From the remaining yellow print fat quarter, cut:
- Four 2" squares
- Four 2½" squares
- Three 2½" x 4½" rectangles

From the remaining blue print fat quarter, cut:
- Six 2½" squares
- Two 4½" x 6½" rectangles
- One 2½" x 6½" rectangle

From the remaining pink print fat quarter, cut:
- Two 2½" x 4½" rectangles
- One 6½" x 14½" rectangle

From the brown print fat quarter, cut:
- One 2½" square
- Two 2½" x 8½" rectangles
- Four 2½" x 6½" rectangles
- Eight 2½" x 4½" rectangles

Quilt originally appeared in *Creative New Quilts & Projects from Precuts or Stash*

Making the Blocks

1. Sew a 2½" x 4½" brown print rectangle to opposite sides of a 2½" x 4½" yellow print rectangle as shown to make Unit A. Make two Units A.

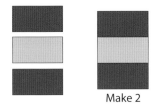

Make 2

2. Draw a diagonal line on the wrong side of the 2½" yellow print squares. With right sides together, place one marked square on a corner of a 2½" x 6½" brown print rectangle.

3. Stitch on the drawn line. Trim ¼" away from the sewn line. Press open to reveal the yellow corner triangle. Repeat on the other end of the brown print rectangle to complete Unit B. Make two Units B.

Make 2

4. Sew Unit B to the right side of Unit A. Carefully watch the orientation of Unit B. Make two of these.

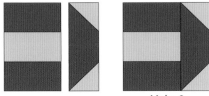

Make 2

5. Draw a diagonal line on the wrong side of the 2" yellow print squares. With right sides together, place one marked square on a corner of a 2½" x 6½" brown print rectangle. Stitch on the drawn line. Trim ¼" away from sewn line. Press open to reveal the yellow corner triangle. Repeat on the other end of the brown print rectangle to complete Unit C. Make two Units C.

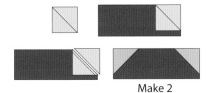

Make 2

6. Sew Unit C to the left side of the unit in Step 4. Carefully watch the orientation of Unit C. Make two.

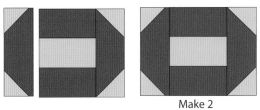

Make 2

7. Draw a diagonal line on the wrong side of the 2½" blue print squares. With right sides together, place one marked square on a corner of a 2½" x 4½" brown print rectangle.

8. Stitch on the drawn line. Trim ¼" away from sewn line. Press open to reveal the blue corner triangle to complete Unit D. Repeat to make another Unit D the mirror image of the first.

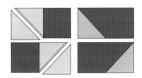

9. Sew Unit D to the right side of one 4½" x 6½" blue print rectangle and to the left side of the other 4½" x 6½" blue print rectangle. Carefully watch the orientation of Unit D.

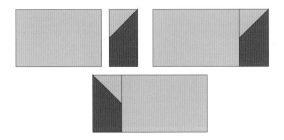

10. Draw a diagonal line on the wrong side of the 2½" blue print squares. With right sides together, place one marked square on a corner of a 2½" x 8½" brown print rectangle.

11. Stitch on the drawn line. Trim ¼" away from sewn line. Press open to reveal the blue corner triangle. Repeat on the other end of the brown print rectangle sewing the second blue print square parallel to the first one. Press open to complete Unit E. Make two of Unit E.

Make 2

12. Sew Unit E to the units made in Step 9.

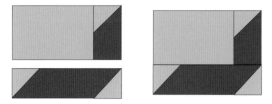

13. Sew the Step 6 and Step 12 units together as shown. The 2" corner triangles are on the outside of the unit. Repeat to make another unit the mirror image of the first.

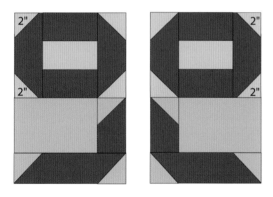

14. Sew a 2½" x 4½" yellow print rectangle, 2½" brown print square, and 2½" x 6½" blue print rectangle together in a column as shown.

15. Sew the column and units from Step 13 together as shown to complete the top section of the block.

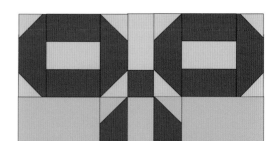

16. Sew the 2½" x 4½" pink print rectangles and 2½" x 4½" brown print rectangles together using diagonal seams as shown. One should be the mirror image of the other.

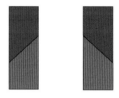

17. Sew the units from Step 16 to opposite sides of the 6½" x 14½" pink print rectangle to complete the bottom section of the block.

18. Sew the top and bottom block sections together to complete the block.

Quilt Top Assembly

1. Lay out eighteen 2½" x 10½" assorted print rectangles in a horizontal row. Sew the rectangles together to make a pieced strip. Make two pieced strips.

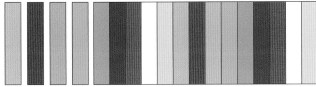

Make 2

2. Lay out the yellow, blue and pink print 6½" x 14½" rectangles in a column as shown. Sew the rectangles together to make Column A.

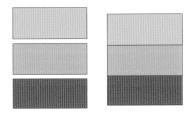

3. Lay out the yellow, blue and pink print 4½" x 6½" rectangles in a column as shown. Sew the rectangles together to make Column B.

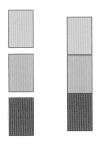

4. Lay out Column A, the block, and Column B as shown. Sew the pieces together to complete the quilt top center section.

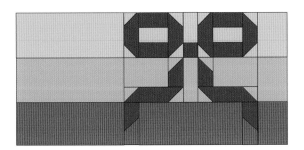

5. Referring to the quilt top assembly diagram, lay out the pieced strips, quilt top center section and sashing strips as shown.

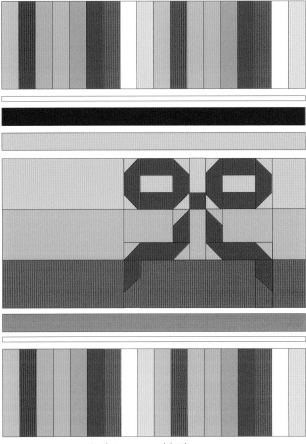

Quilt top assembly diagram

Finishing

1. Lay the backing fabric wrong side up on a flat surface. The backing fabric should be taut. Place the batting on the backing and the quilt top on the batting, right side up, to form a quilt sandwich. Baste the quilt sandwich.

2. Quilt as desired. A swirly vine with variations was used on the featured quilt.

3. Sew the five 2½" x WOF binding strips together along the short ends to make one continuous binding strip. Fold the piece in half lengthwise, wrong sides together, and press. Sew to the raw edge of the quilt top. Fold the binding over the raw edges and hand stitch in place on back of quilt.

Childhood Memories with Sailboat Block

By Wendy Sheppard

Finished quilt size: Approximately 36" x 45" (91 x 114cm)

This twist on the Childhood Memories quilt features sunny florals and a colorful sailboat.

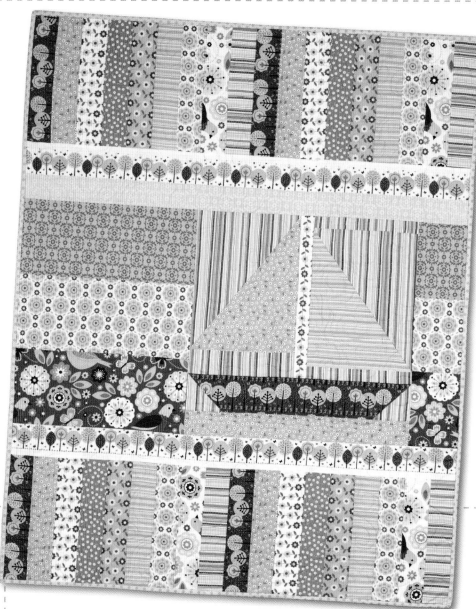

Block Materials

Note: Refer to page 20 (Childhood Memories) for additional materials and cutting instructions for the rest of the quilt.

- One orange stripe fat quarter
- One blue stripe fat quarter
- One blue print fat quarter
- One floral print fat quarter **or** one 1½" x 13½" scrap piece
- One tree print fat quarter

Fat quarter = 18" x 22"

Quilt originally appeared in *Creative New Quilts & Projects from Precuts or Stash*

Cutting

Note: If you are using a directional print fabric similar to the stripe fabric used in the sailboat block, pay special attention when cutting the fabric.

From the orange stripe fat quarter, cut:

- Two 9¼" x 12" rectangles. Cut each rectangle in half diagonally to make four half-rectangle triangles. Choose two half-rectangles with stripes going in same direction for the block.

Note: If print fabric isn't directional, you will only need one 9¼" x 12" rectangle.

- Two 1½" x 9" rectangles
- One 2½" x 9" rectangle
- Two 3½" squares

From the blue stripe fat quarter, cut:

- One 9¼" x 12" rectangle. Cut the rectangle in half diagonally to make two half-rectangle triangles. You will only need one.

From the blue print fat quarter, cut:

- One 9¼" x 12" rectangle. Cut the rectangle in half diagonally to make two half-rectangle triangles. You will only need one.
- One 2½" x 18½" rectangle

From the floral print fat quarter, cut:

- One 1½" x 13½" rectangle

From the tree print fat quarter, cut:

- One 3½" x 18½" rectangle

Block Assembly

1. Layer an orange stripe half-rectangle triangle and a blue print half-rectangle triangle, right sides together. Sew the pieces together along the long edge. Press open to make Unit A.

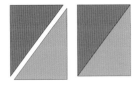

2. Sew a 2½" x 9½" orange stripe rectangle to the bottom of Unit A to make the left section of the block.

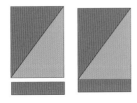

3. Layer an orange stripe half-rectangle triangle and a blue stripe half-rectangle triangle, right sides together. Sew the pieces together along the long edge. Press open to make Unit B.

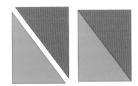

4. Sew 1½" x 9½" orange stripe rectangles to the top and bottom of Unit B to make the right section of the block.

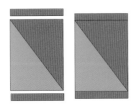

5. Sew the left and right sections of the block to opposite sides of the 1½" x 13½" floral print rectangle to complete the block's top section.

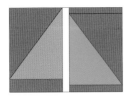

6. Draw a diagonal line on the wrong side of the 3½" orange stripe squares. Pay attention to the direction of the stripes. With right sides together, place a marked square at a corner of a 3½" x 18½" tree print rectangle.

7. Stitch on the drawn line. Trim ¼" away from sewn line. Press open to reveal the orange stripe corner triangle. Repeat on the other end of the tree print rectangle. Press open to complete Unit C.

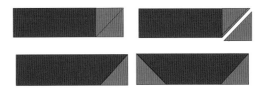

8. Sew a 2½" x 18½" blue print rectangle to the bottom of Unit C to complete the block's bottom section.

9. Sew the top and bottom block sections together to complete the block.

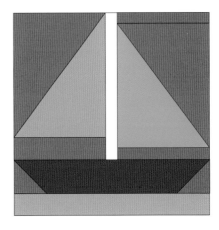

10. Refer to page 23 (Childhood Memories) for quilt assembly and finishing instructions.

Springtime for Baby

By Janet Pittman
Finished size: 36" x 36" (91 x 91cm)

Turn puzzle blocks into a flannel quilt in bright pastels as a cozy welcome for a new arrival.

Materials
- 1½ yards yellow print flannel for blocks, border, and binding
- One fat quarter each of turquoise, green, and yellow tone-on-tone flannel prints for puzzle blocks
- ½ yard paper-backed fusible web
- 1¼ yards flannel backing fabric
- 42" x 42" batting (or crib-size batting)

Fabric suggestions are 40"–42" wide.

Fat quarter = 18" x 20"

Sew all patchwork seams with a ¼" seam allowance.

Follow the manufacturer's directions for using paper-backed fusible web.

Cutting

From the yellow print, cut:
- Four 2½" strips for binding
- Two 5" x 36½" side borders, see tip below
- Two 5" x 27½" top and bottom borders
- Eighteen 5" squares

From each tone-on-tone fat quarter cut
- Six 5" squares

Crosswise

2½" for binding

Top border

Bottom border

Lengthwise

Side border

Side border

For Directional Fabric

If fabric is directional, cut two 5"-wide **lengthwise** strips after cutting the binding strips. Then cut the remaining fabric into 5"-wide crosswise strips.

Quilt originally appeared in *Colorful Quilts for Playful Kids*

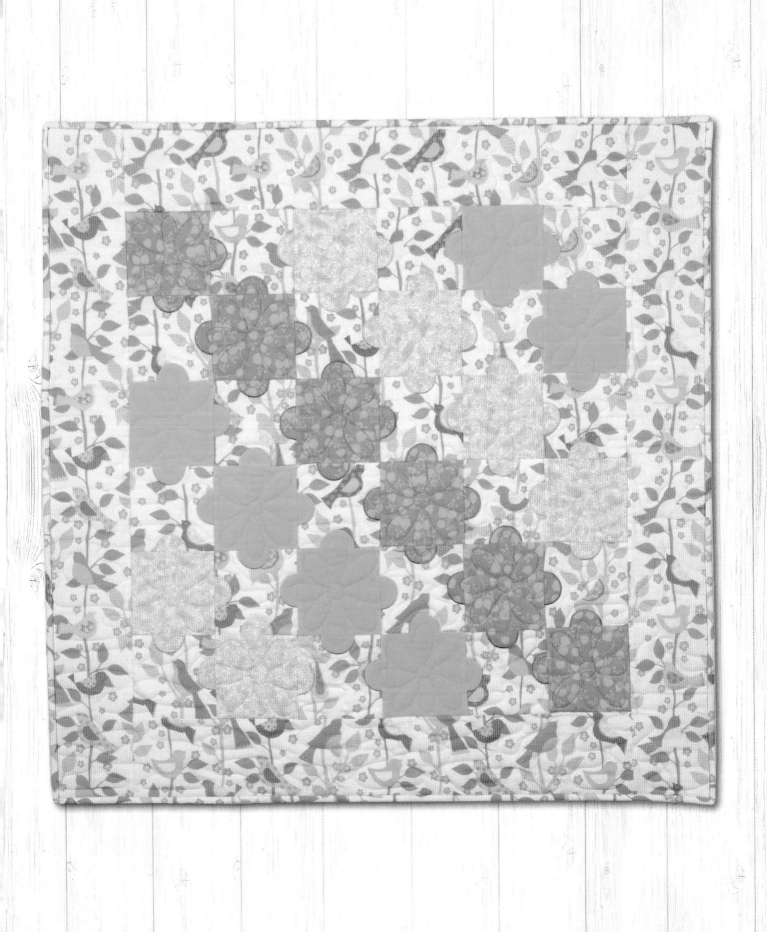

Preparing the Appliqué Pieces

Following the instructions in Preparing Fused Appliqué on page 29, make the following appliqué pieces. The puzzle tab template is found on page 150.

- Twenty turquoise puzzle tabs
- Twenty yellow puzzle tabs
- Twenty green puzzle tabs

Stitching the Appliqué

1. Referring to the chart below, position the puzzle tabs on yellow print squares, aligning the straight edge of the puzzle tab with the edge of the yellow square. The puzzle tabs are centered on the sides of the yellow print squares. Fuse in place.

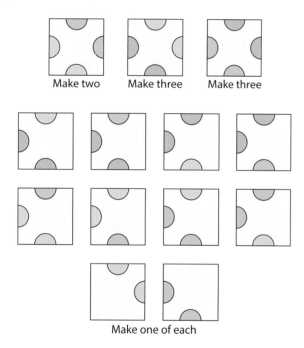

Make two   Make three   Make three

Make one of each

Note: Work on a non-stick pressing sheet to protect your pressing surface.

2. Stitch the curved edge of each puzzle tab with a satin zigzag stitch, using thread that matches the tabs.

Quilt Top Assembly

1. Arrange the blocks and the turquoise, yellow, and green squares as shown.

2. Join into rows, then join the rows to complete the quilt center.

3. Sew the yellow print top and bottom borders to the quilt center. Sew the yellow print side borders to the quilt.

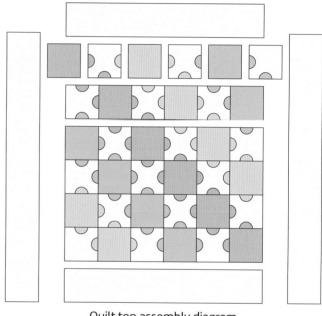

Quilt top assembly diagram

Finishing

1. Layer the quilt top, batting, and backing.

2. Quilt as desired.

3. Trim the excess batting and backing to straighten the edges and square the corners.

4. Stitch together the yellow print 2½"-wide strips with diagonal seams to make a continuous strip. Use to bind the quilt; see instructions starting on page 58 or page 64.

Preparing Fused Appliqué

Paper-backed fusible web can be used for any machine appliqué. It is especially useful for shapes with intricate edges that would be difficult to turn under. The placement line is indicated by a dashed line on the puzzle tab template.

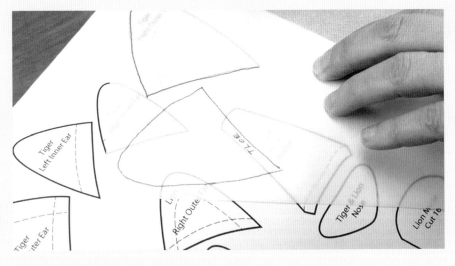

1. Place lightweight paper-backed fusible web with the paper side up on the appliqué template. Using an ultra-fine tip permanent marker or pencil, trace each template piece onto the paper side of the fusible web. Mark the template name near an edge of the template.

2. Trace the appliqué pieces that will be cut from the same fabric about ⅛" apart.

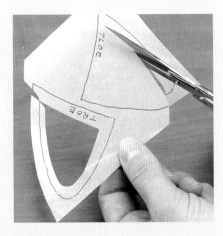

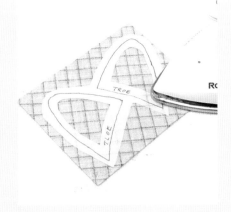

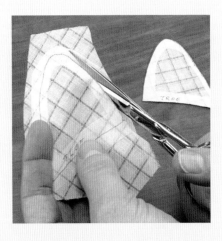

3. If desired, remove the fusible web from the center of the larger template pieces. Cut through an outer edge into the center of the template. Cut out the center, leaving a scant ¼" inside the traced line. This makes the appliqué center softer to the touch and in appearance. This technique is frequently called "windowing."

4. Cut away the excess fusible web about ⅛" from the traced lines. Fuse templates to the wrong side of the fabric, following the manufacturer's directions. Each brand of fusible web comes with instructions that detail pressing times and iron temperatures.

5. Cut out the fused appliqué pieces on the traced line. Do not remove the paper backing until just before arranging the pieces for pressing to the background. This preserves the template name. If you are working with hand-dyed or batik fabrics, and it is hard to tell the right from the wrong side of the fabric, this will also help indicate which side has the glue. It also prevents a gummed-up iron surface.

Baby Quilt

Designed by Suzanne McNeill, pieced and quilted by Osie Lebowitz
Finished size: 28" x 32½" (71 x 83cm)

Has your guild or sewing circle been searching for a fabulous and fast quilt? Look no further. Welcome the newest family member with this wonderful quilt and create an heirloom that will be treasured for generations to come.

Materials

- ⅓ yard white dot fabric to cut ten squares
- ⅓ yard white print fabric to cut ten squares
- ⅙ yard turquoise solid fabric for appliqués
- 4" x 13" red fabric for apple and hearts
- 8" x 8" gold fabric for bear and duck
- 6" x 6" dark brown fabric for bear
- 2" x 6" yellow fabric for butterfly body
- ¼ yard red print fabric for Border 1 and connections
- ⅝ yard turquoise print fabric for Border 2 and binding
- 1 yard backing fabric
- 36" x 41" batting
- Black embroidery floss, chenille needle
- Fusible web (such as Steam-A-Seam 2®) for appliqués
- AccuQuilt® GO! Me® fabric cutter and the following dies (or template plastic and templates on pages 150–151):
- GO! die #55010 Square 5"
- GO! die #55030 Critters
- GO! die #55012 Circles 2", 3", 5"
- GO! die #55035 Alpha Baby
- GO! die #55037 Baby, Baby
- GO! die #55029 Hearts 2", 3", 4"
- GO! die #55331 Stems & Leaves

Quilt originally appeared in *GO! Baby® Quilting*

Cutting

Die cut all pieces as listed or, if you are not using the fabric cutter, trace the templates onto the fabric as indicated and cut out the appliqués.

- #55010 Square 5"
  - White dots: ten
  - White print: ten

Note: Apply fusible web to the back of fabrics before cutting the appliqués.

- #55030 Critters
  - Turquoise solid: one butterfly wings
  - Yellow: one butterfly body
- #55012 Circle 3"
  - Red solid: one for peach
- #55035 Alpha Baby
  - Turquoise solid: letters B, A, B, Y
- #55037 Baby, Baby
  - Gold: one duck, two bear ears, two bear eyebrows, four paw pads
  - Turquoise: one duck eye, one duck wing, two bear eyes, one bear nose, one bow tie
  - Dark brown: one bear
  - Red: one duck bill
- #55029 Heart 3"
  - Red: two hearts
- #55331 Stems & Leaves
  - Turquoise solid: two leaves for peach
  - Dark brown: one stem for peach

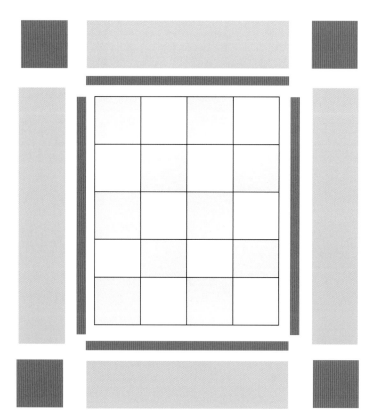

Quilt top assembly diagram

Quilt Top Assembly

1. Refer to the quilt assembly diagram.

2. Arrange the pieces on a work surface.

3. Arrange five rows of four squares each, alternating the prints. Press.

4. Sew the rows together. Press.

Adding Appliqués

1. Press the appliqués onto their background squares. Appliqué as desired.

2. Embroider antennae on the butterfly.

Border 1

1. Cut two strips 1½"x 23" for sides.

2. Cut two strips 1½" x 20½" for top and bottom.

3. Sew side borders to the quilt. Press.

4. Sew top and bottom borders to the quilt. Press.

Border 2

1. Cut two strips 4½" x 25" for sides.

2. Cut two strips 4½" x 20½" for top and bottom.

3. Cut four red print cornerstones 4½" x 4½". Sew one to each end of the top and bottom strips.

4. Sew side borders to the quilt. Press.

5. Sew top and bottom borders to the quilt. Press.

Finishing

1. Quilt as desired and bind the edges.

2. Sew 2½" strips together end to end to equal 132".

3. Follow the binding instructions starting on page 58 or page 64.

Appliqué placement diagram

Little Schoolhouse

By McB McManus and E.B. Updegraff
Finished size: Approximately
30" x 36" (76 x 91cm)

With a mix of pastel shades
and bright hues in its sixteen-
patch and four-patch blocks,
this cheerful design has
plenty of contrast to grab
baby's attention. It could
even add a charming pop
of color to the décor of a
preschooler's room.

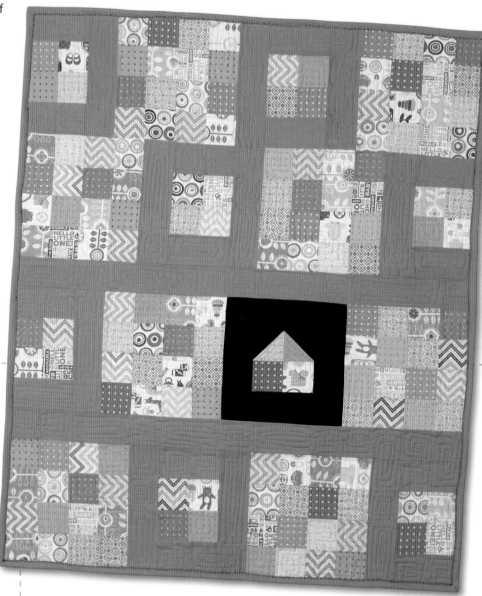

Materials

- Forty-one 5" assorted print
  squares or one charm pack
  with a minimum of forty-
  one squares
- ¾ yard green solid fabric
- One fat eighth purple
  solid fabric
- 1¼ yards backing fabric
- ⅓ yard binding fabric
- 34" x 40" batting

WOF = width of fabric
Fabric quantities based on
42"–44"-wide, 100% cotton
Charm pack = 5" squares

*Quilt originally appeared in Easy-
Cut Baby Quilts*

Cutting

From assorted 5" print
squares, cut:
- 159 2½" squares

Note: Cut each 5" square in half
twice to get four 2½" squares.
- One 3⅜" square

From the green solid fabric, cut:
- Six 2½" x WOF strips. From
  four of the strips, subcut:
  - Fourteen 2½" x 4½"
    rectangles
  - Ten 2½" x 8½" rectangles

Set the two remaining strips aside
for sashing.

From the purple solid fabric, cut:
- Two 2½" x 4½" rectangles
- Two 2½" x 8½" rectangles
- One 3⅜" square

From the binding fabric, cut:
- Four 2½" x WOF strips

Making the Blocks

Sixteen-Patch Blocks

1. Lay out sixteen assorted 2½" print squares in four rows with four squares in each row as shown.

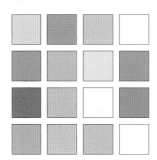

2. Sew the squares together in rows. Sew the rows together to complete the sixteen-patch block. Make a total of eight sixteen-patch blocks.

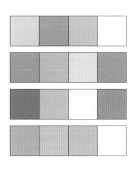
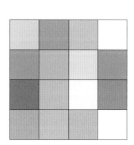

Make eight

Four-Patch Blocks

1. Lay out four assorted 2½" print squares as shown. Sew the squares together to make a four-patch block. Make a total of seven four-patch blocks.

Make seven

2. Sew 2½" x 4½" green solid rectangles to the top and bottom of the four-patch block.

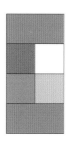

3. Sew a 2½" x 8½" green solid rectangle to one side of the four-patch blocks. Set four of the blocks aside.

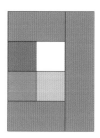

4. Sew 2½" x 8½" green solid rectangles to opposite sides of the three remaining four-patch blocks.

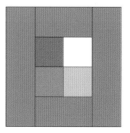

Size Twist

For charming, coordinated nursery décor, make additional blocks and frame them.

House Block

Note: The featured quilt uses two different prints in the half-square triangles for a scrappier look. The instructions use one print.

1. Sew two assorted 2½" print squares together as shown.

2. Layer the 3⅜" print square on the 3⅜" solid purple square, right sides together. Draw a diagonal line from corner to corner on the wrong side of the print square.

3. Sew a ¼" on either side of the drawn line. Cut on the drawn line and press the pieces open to create two half-square triangles.

4. Sew the half-square triangles together as shown.

5. Sew the squares from Step 1 and the half-square triangle set together as shown to make the block center.

6. Sew 2½" x 4½" purple solid rectangles to the top and bottom of the block center. Sew 2½" x 8½" purple solid rectangles to the remaining sides of the block center to complete the house block.

Quilt Top Assembly

1. Referring to the quilt top assembly diagram, lay out the blocks and sashing strips as shown.

2. Sew the blocks together in rows. Sew the rows and sashing strips together to complete the quilt top.

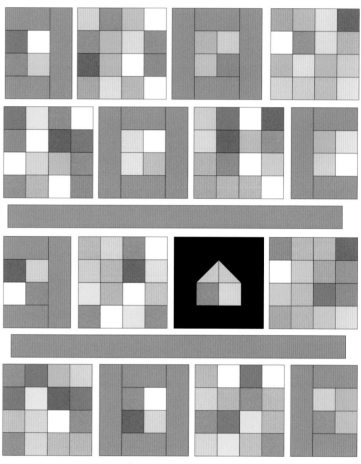

Quilt top assembly diagram

Finish the Quilt

1. Square up the quilt top.

2. Layer the backing, batting, and quilt top. Baste the layers together and hand- or machine-quilt as desired.

3. Sew the 2½"-wide binding strips together to make one continuous strip. Press the strip in half lengthwise, wrong sides together. Sew the binding to the front of the quilt, aligning the raw edges. Turn the binding over the edge to the back of the quilt and hand- or machine-stitch in place.

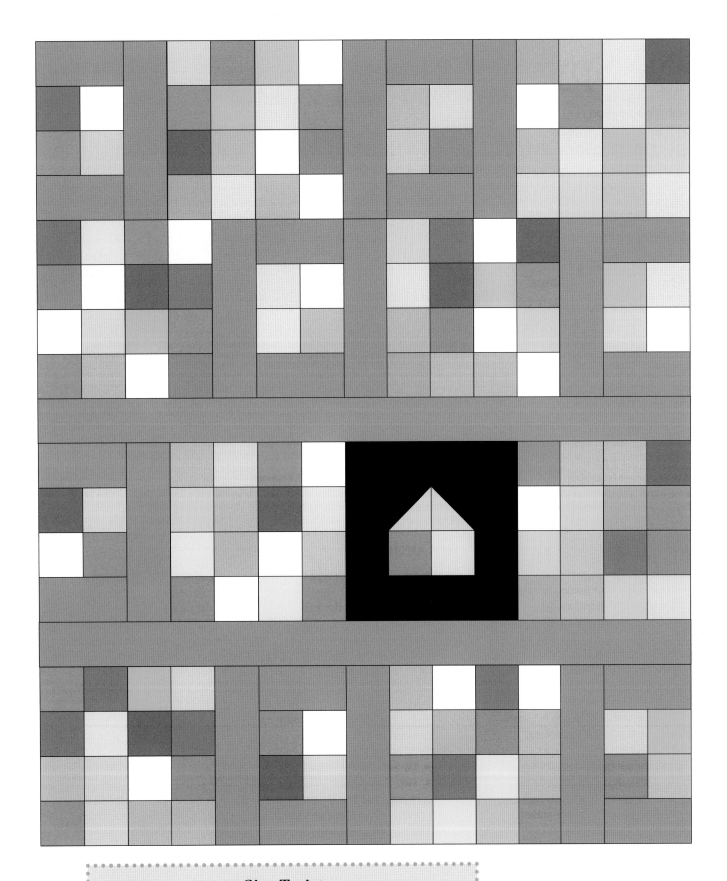

Size Twist

- Sew four sixteen-patch blocks together to make a doll quilt.
- Sew the two top or bottom rows together to make a play quilt.

Eye Spy

By Phyllis Anderson
Finished size: Approximately
   36½" x 44½" (93 x 113cm)

Eye Spy is a wonderful learning quilt for children. Using novelty prints, fussy cut the rhombus units with the Creative Grids® Sweet 'N Sassy Templates™ Rhombus #2 (see page 156).

Materials

- Assorted novelty prints (113 rhombus units needed)
- ½ yard navy print for setting units and corner triangles
- ¼ yard green print for inner border
- ¾ yard red print for outer border and binding
- 1½ yards backing
- 43" x 51" batting
- Creative Grids® Sweet 'N Sassy Templates™ Rhombus #2 or template material and template on page 156

Note: Do **not** fold the fabric strips in half when cutting with the rhombus template. Use only a single-layer strip. The template has registration lines on all four sides as well as ¼" seam allowance "holes" for marking.

Quantities are based on 42"-wide fabric. Measurements include ¼" seam allowances. Sew with right sides together unless otherwise stated.

WOF = width of fabric

Quilt originally appeared in *Sweet 'N Sassy Templates™ Diamond Quilts*

Cutting

Press all fabrics before you begin cutting and remove selvages.

Note: Many novelty prints contain a multitude of usable motifs. Select motifs that fit within the seam lines of the rhombus template. Before cutting along the edges of the template, center it over an individual motif as shown below or position it as desired on an all-over patterned fabric.

From assorted novelty prints, cut:
- 113 rhombus units, using each motif once

From navy print, cut:
- Two 4⅜" x WOF strips
- Two 3⅝" squares, cutting each in half diagonally once for a total of four corner triangles

From green print, cut:
- Four 1½" x WOF inner border strips

From red print, cut:
- Four 3½" x WOF outer border strips
- Four 2¼" x WOF binding strips

Rhombus template

Cutting the Setting Units

1. Place a navy 4⅜" x WOF strip in a single layer on your cutting mat. Position the rhombus template on the strip and butt the edge of a 24" ruler against the left edge of the template to achieve the correct angle. Slide the template away and cut along the right edge of the ruler.

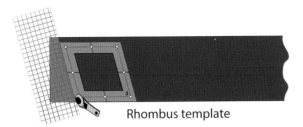
Rhombus template

2. Move the template over 1" from the angled edge of the fabric and cut a rhombus unit. Repeat to cut a total of fourteen rhombus units from the two strips.

Note: Your rhombus units are 1" larger than your template because you will need the extra length and width for the setting units to fit properly.

3. Position seven rhombus units as shown and cut in half widthwise for a total of fourteen top and bottom setting units.

Make fourteen top and bottom setting units

4. Position seven rhombus units as shown and cut in half lengthwise for a total of fourteen side setting units.

Make fourteen side setting units

Quilt Center Assembly

1. Referring to the quilt center assembly diagram, lay out the rhombus units and the top, bottom, and side setting units in diagonal rows on a flat surface or design wall. The corner triangles will be added later.

Quilt center assembly diagram

2. Beginning in the upper left-hand corner, flip the rhombus unit onto the side setting unit with right sides together. The units will not align perfectly and the setting unit will overhang ¼". Sew the units together.

3. Flip the top setting unit onto the rhombus unit from the previous step. Sew the units together to complete the first row. Press all seams toward the top setting unit.

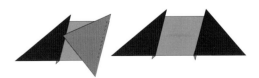

4. Mark the wrong side of the rhombus units in the second diagonal row. Place the rhombus template over each unit and mark the center ¼" seam allowance dot on the left and right edges. Reposition each rhombus unit right side up in the row.

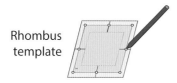

Rhombus template

5. Following the method in Step 2, join the side setting unit and the first rhombus unit in the second row.

6. Lay the next rhombus unit on the rhombus unit from Step 5 with right sides together. Take a straight pin and push it through the dots on both units. Make sure the pin stays straight and the edges are aligned where the dots meet. The rhombus units will not be aligned. Pin the units together and sew. Repeat this process for the remaining rhombus units in the row.

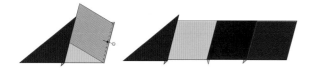

7. Attach the top setting unit to the last rhombus unit. Continue in this same manner to mark and complete the second diagonal row. Press all seams in this row toward the side setting unit.

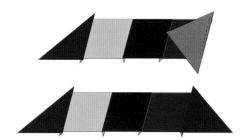

8. Continue in this manner to mark and sew the units together in diagonal rows. Press the seams in one direction, alternating the direction from row to row.

Note: After each row is sewn together, place it back in position on the flat surface or design wall.

9. Turn over the first and second rows to mark the wrong side. Place the rhombus template over each rhombus unit and mark the ¼" seam allowance dot on the seams of both rows.

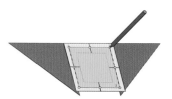

10. Lay the first row on the second row with right sides together. Pin the rows together, pushing a straight pin through the seam allowance dots on both rows. Make sure the pin stays straight and the edges are aligned where the dots meet. Sew the rows together and press the seam in one direction.

Note: The two rows will not nest together because they are rhombus shapes.

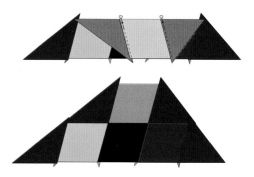

11. Continue in this same manner to mark and sew the rows together. Press the seams in one direction. Center and sew the navy print corner triangles to the corners of the quilt center; press the seams toward the triangles.

12. Use a rotary cutter and acrylic ruler to trim all edges of the quilt center ¼" beyond the outermost point of the rhombus units.

Adding the Borders

1. Measure top to bottom through the middle of your quilt center and also near the left and right edges. Add these measurements together and divide by three. Use this number to cut two inner border strips from the green print 1½" inner border strips. Sew the strips to the left and right edges of the quilt center, easing the strips to fit.

2. Measure side to side through the middle of your quilt center and near the top and bottom, including the side inner border in your measurements. Add these measurements together and divide by three. Use this number to cut two inner border strips from the green print 1½" inner border strips. Sew strips to the top and bottom edges of the quilt center, easing to fit.

3. Repeat Steps 1–2 with the red print 3½" outer border strips.

Finishing

1. Layer the quilt top, batting, and backing.

2. Quilt as desired.

3. Bind with red print binding strips; follow the binding instructions starting on page 58 or page 64.

Quilt top assembly diagram

Sweet Dreams under Starry Skies

By Carol C. Porter and Rebecca J. Hansen
Finished size: 36½" x 60½" (93 x 154cm)

Sweet dreams will surely spring to life under the warmth of this quilt. Wrap up your little one and get cozy in a rocker by the fireplace, on the porch, or in the nursery . . . it's time to tell stories and create memories.

The beauty of this quilt is the unexpected fracturing of the upper section. A Summer Winds block placed on point represents the moon. The twirling effect that surrounds this block, created by using pinwheels and yellow and peach colors, gives a sense of twinkling stars. Parts of the Milky Way block peek through at the corners of this section. The middle of the quilt contains Port and Starboard blocks to settle the mood, and the quilt ends with Nautilus blocks along the bottom. The entire quilt makes you wonder if Wynken, Blynken, and Nod are there somewhere under the starry skies.

Materials

This quilt is all about color values. Using the values of dark, medium, medium-light, and light sets the mood and movement of the design. The darks and mediums of the purple, green, and blue of the sky set against the light yellows and peaches make the eye focus on the moon and stars. The use of medium-light to medium with a smattering of dark and a dash of light give the Port and Starboard area a more calming sea, while the darks, mediums, medium-lights, and lights promote the movement and foaming of the waves.

As you select your fabrics, consider using some batiks and hand-dyes, as these often have good transitions between colors, such as from yellow to peach and blue to green.

From the color palette of purple, blue, and green, select values as follows:
- Eleven fat quarters dark fabrics
- Thirteeen fat quarters medium and medium-light fabrics
- Three fat quarters light fabrics

From the color palette of yellow and peach, select values as follows:
- Three fat quarters light to bright yellow fabrics
- One fat quarter light to medium yellow/peach batik fabric
- Four fat quarters light peach fabric
- One fat quarter dark peach/green batik fabric

½ yard striped fabric for binding
Batting and backing fabric

The splashes of yellow and peach in this quilt give the impression of twinkling stars or the sky at sunset.

Quilt originally appeared in *Seaside Quilts*

Cutting and Making the Blocks

Summer Winds Block

1. Cut four 2½" x 2½" squares from the blue-green batik for the corners.

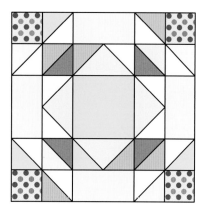

2. Cut four 2½" x 4½" rectangles from yellow.

3. Cut one 4" x 4" square from yellow for the center.

4. Cut four 2½" x 4" rectangles and eight 2½" x 2½" squares from yellows and peaches. Make four Flying Geese units (see page 46).

5. Cut six 2⅞" x 2⅞" squares from yellows and six 2⅞" x 2⅞" squares from peaches. Make twelve half-square triangle units (see page 45).

6. Lay out the block and stitch the pieces into rows. Then stitch the rows together as illustrated below. Trim the block to 12" x 12". The finished size will be 11½". Make one Summer Winds block.

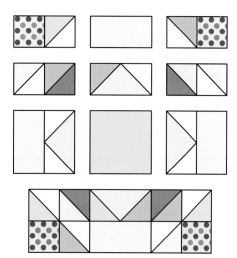

Nautilus Block

1. From the purple, blue, and green palette, cut three light, three medium-light, three medium, and three dark squares, each 2⅝" x 2⅝". Use one square from each value to make three four-patch units (see page 45). Trim the units to 4¼".

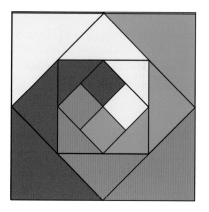

2. Cut two 3⅞" x 3⅞" squares from each of the four values (for a total of eight squares), then crosscut them diagonally once. Sew one triangle of each value to the four-patch from Step 1. Trim the unit to 6½".

3. Cut two 4⅞" x 4⅞" squares from each of the four values (for a total of eight squares), then crosscut them diagonally once. Sew one triangle of each value to the unit made in Step 2. Trim the unit to 9".

4. Cut two 6⅞" x 6⅞" squares from each of the four values (for a total of eight squares), and then crosscut them diagonally once. Sew one triangle of each value to the unit made in Step 3. Trim the unit to 12½". The finished size of the unit will be 12". Make three Nautilus blocks.

5. Sew the three Nautilus blocks into a row.

Port and Starboard Block

1. From the purple, blue, and green palette, choose eight assorted fabrics from the medium/medium-light fabric values and cut eighteen squares, each 4⅞" x 4⅞". Crosscut these squares diagonally once, and divide them by color into medium and medium-light stacks.

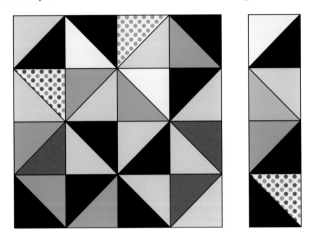

2. From the same palette, choose eight assorted fabrics from the dark fabric values and cut fifteen squares, each 4⅞" x 4⅞". Crosscut these squares diagonally once, and place them in a stack.

3. From the same palette, choose two assorted fabrics from the light fabric values and cut three squares, each 4⅞" x 4⅞". Crosscut these squares diagonally once, and place them in a stack.

4. From the stacks, make thirty-six half-square triangle units. Arrange and sew the units as illustrated into two blocks and one filler strip. Trim blocks to 16½". The finished size of the blocks will be 16".

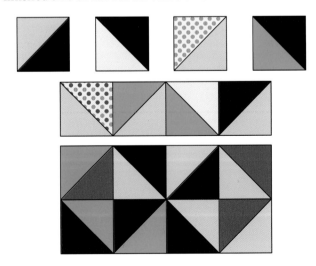

5. Sew the two blocks and filler strip into a row.

Top Section

The best way to approach the design work for this section is to place the Summer Winds block on point on a design wall. Cut and sew the following units, place them around the Summer Winds block, and then sew the units together in sections as shown in the quilt top assembly diagram on page 47.

Four-Patch Unit

1. From the purple, blue, and green palette, cut forty 2½" x 2½" squares.

2. Make ten four-patch units. Trim them to 4½".

Half-Square Triangle Unit

1. From the purple, blue, and green palette, cut seventeen 4⅞" x 4⅞" squares, then crosscut them diagonally once.

2. Make fifteen half-square triangle units (leave four triangles unsewn; see page 44). Trim them to 4½".

Pinwheel Unit

1. Cut five assorted yellow, eleven assorted peach, and twenty-three assorted green/purple/blue squares, each 3⅞" x 3⅞". Crosscut the squares diagonally once. Make twenty-seven half-square triangle units and trim them to 3½".

2. From the half-square triangle units, make six pinwheels (you will use four half-square triangle units for each pinwheel). Trim them to 6½".

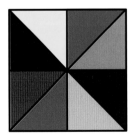

3. Make two half-pinwheel units.

4. Make eight quarter-pinwheel units.

Squares

Cut six 4½" x 4½" squares.

Large Half-Square Triangles

Cut six 6½" squares. Then crosscut the squares diagonally once.

Quilt Top Assembly

1. With the units for the top section cut and sewn, they are now ready to go up on the design wall. Sew the sections together to make large units, and then sew the units together.

2. To complete this quilt, add the Port and Starboard row to the top section. Then add the Nautilus row to the bottom.

Finishing

1. Mark the quilt top for quilting using a design of your choice.

2. Layer the quilt top with the batting and backing; baste it in place.

3. Quilt as desired, and then bind the edges. Follow the binding instructions starting on page 58 or page 64.

4. Add a label, and sign, date, and photograph your finished quilt.

Cutting and Making Flying Geese Units

1. To make the Flying Geese units, cut one rectangle 2" x 3½".

2. Cut two squares each 2" x 2". Draw a diagonal line on each square from corner to corner.

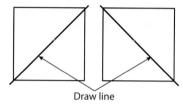

Draw line

3. Place one square on the left side of the rectangle with right sides together; sew on the diagonal line. Trim the seam to ¼" and press the triangle up.

Trim to ¼"

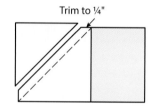

4. Repeat with the second square on the right side of the rectangle.

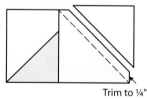

Trim to ¼"

5. The Flying Geese unit should measure 2" x 3½". **Note:** There is some waste with this method; however, many quilters agree that working with squares is easier and faster than working with small triangles.

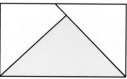

Trim to 2" x 3½"

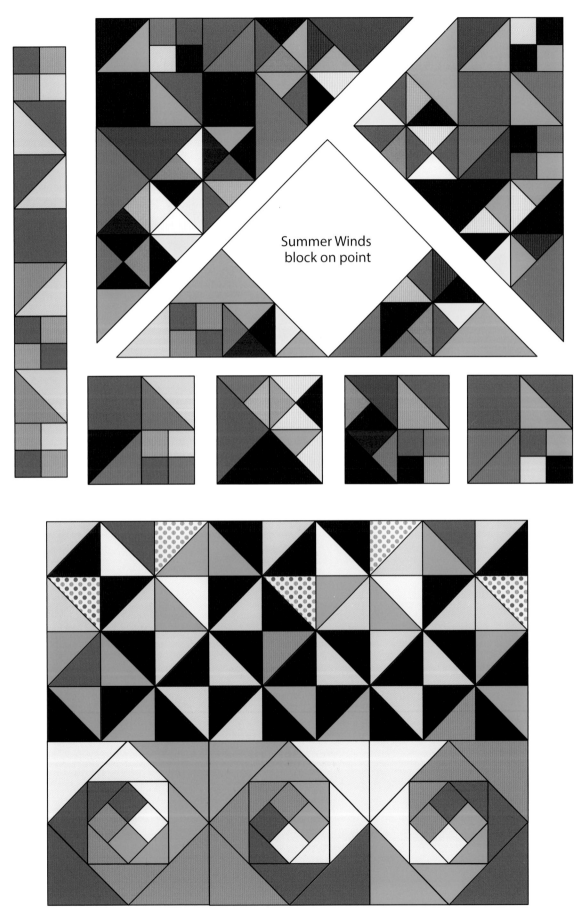

Summer Winds
block on point

Quilt top assembly diagram

Cornered Quilt

By McB McManus and E.B. Updegraff
Finished quilt: Approximately
39" x 45" (99 x 114cm)

The vibrant red and aqua prints against crisp white offer a fresh take on traditional baby pastels. With a quilting motif that echoes the angles of the half-square triangles, the Cornered quilt is the perfect accent to a modern nursery.

Materials

- Two fat eighths in assorted red prints
- Two fat eighths in assorted aqua prints
- 1¾ yards light solid fabric
- 3 yards backing fabric
- ½ yard binding fabric
- 45" x 51" batting

WOF = width of fabric
Fabric quantities based on 42–44"-wide, 100% cotton fabrics
Fat eighth = 9" x 22"

Cutting

From one red print fat eighth, cut:
- One 5" x WOF strip. From the strip, subcut:
  - Four 5" squares

From remaining red print fat eighth, cut:
- One 5" x WOF strip. From the strip, subcut:
  - Two 5" squares

From one aqua print fat eighth, cut:
- One 5" x WOF strip. From the strip, subcut:
  - Three 5" squares

From remaining aqua print fat eighth, cut:
- One 5" x WOF strip. From the strip, subcut:
  - Two 5" squares

From light solid fabric, cut:
- Two 5" x WOF strips. From the strips, subcut:
  - Eleven 5" squares
- Six 4½" x WOF strips. From the strips, subcut:
  - One 4½" x 35" rectangle
  - One 4½" x 31" rectangle
  - One 4½" x 27" rectangle
  - One 4½" x 23" rectangle
  - One 4½" x 19" rectangle
  - One 4½" x 15" rectangle
- One 21½" x WOF rectangle

From binding fabric, cut:
- Five 2½" x WOF strips

Quilt originally appeared in *Easy-Cut Baby Quilts*

Making the Half-Square Triangles

1. Layer a 5" red print square on a 5" light solid square, right sides together.

2. Draw a diagonal line from corner to corner on the wrong side of the red print square. Sew a ¼" on either side of the drawn line.

3. Cut on the drawn line. Press the seam toward the red print fabric to make two half-square triangles. Square each unit to 4-½". Make a total of twelve red print half-square triangles.

Make twelve

4. Referring to Steps 1–3, make a total of ten aqua print half-square triangles. You will use nine.

Make ten

Making the Rows

1. Referring to the diagram for half-square triangle placement and strip length, lay out the bottom six rows as shown.

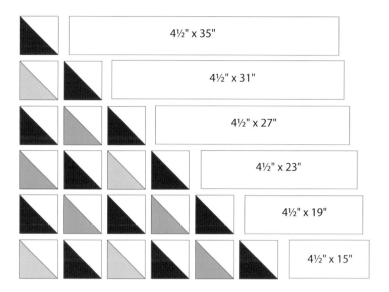

2. Sew the pieces in each row together. Press seams open.

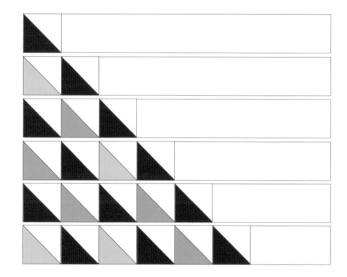

3. Sew the rows together, matching the half-square triangle seams in each row. Press the seams open to complete the bottom section of the quilt top.

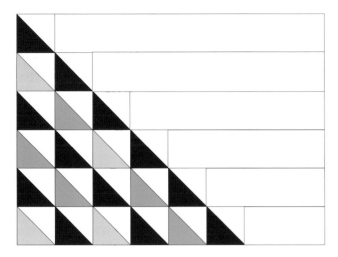

Pillow

Make a pillow by sewing nine half-square triangles together in three rows. Repeat to make the pillow back or use a solid piece of fabric.
Approximate size: 12" x 12"

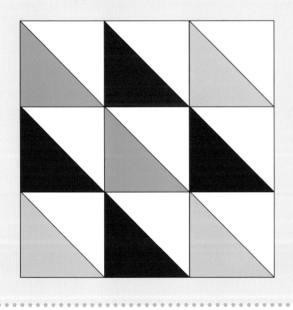

Quilt Top Assembly

1. With right sides together, sew the light solid 21½" x WOF rectangle to the bottom section of the quilt top. Press seams open.

2. Trim the top section even with the bottom section to square up the quilt top.

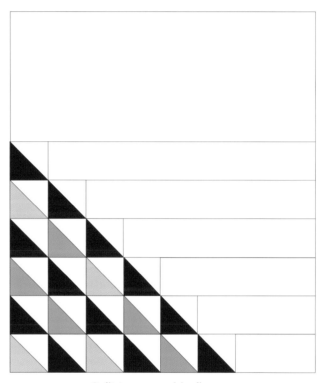

Quilt top assembly diagram

Finish the Quilt

1. Layer the backing, batting, and quilt top. Baste the layers together and hand- or machine-quilt as desired.

2. Sew the 2½"-wide binding strips together to make one continuous strip. Press the strip in half lengthwise, wrong sides together. Sew the binding to the front of the quilt, aligning the raw edges. Turn the binding over the edge to the back of the quilt and hand- or machine-stitch in place.

Fun in the Sun

Designed by Suzanne McNeill, pieced by
Kayleen Allen, quilted by Sue Needle
Finished size: 28" x 37" (71 x 94cm)

The fabrics for this happy little
baby quilt are inspired by nature's
own graphics. Clamshells, daisies,
orchid petals, wandering vines, and
raindrop patterns on water combine
to create a soothing setting for a
crib quilt or wall hanging. The
techniques are easily
expanded to larger
sizes, so the
whole family
can enjoy this
fabulous design.

These
instructions are
for a newborn baby
quilt, size 28" x 37".
(Refer to the chart
below for other
sizes.)

Choose a Quilt Size

	Color	Location	YARDAGE			
			Throw 48" x 67"	**Double** 67" x 86"	**King** 113" x 113"	**Baby** 28" x 37"
Fabric A	Assorted light prints	Corners	1¾ yards	3⅜ yards	7 yards	⅝ yard
Fabric B	Dark print	Centers	⅝ yard	1½ yards	3⅛ yards	⅓ yard
Fabric C	Light print	Border #1	¼ yard	⅓ yard	¾ yard	⅙ yard
Fabric D	Medium large print	Border 2 and binding	1¾ yards	2¼ yards	3¼ yards	⅔ yard
	Cut size	**Location**				
Fabric A	10" x 10"	Corners	Twenty-four light print	Forty-eight light print	100 light print	Twenty-four light print
Fabric B	10" x 10"	Centers	8 dark print	18 dark print	41 dark print	8 dark print
Fabric A	5" x 5"	Corners	Two 1½" x 57½"	Two 1½" x 76½"	Two 2½" x 95½"	Two 1½" x 27½"
Fabric B	5" x 5"	Centers	Two 1½" x 40½"	Two 1½" x 59½"	Two 2½" x 99½"	Two 1½" x 20½"
		Border 1	Two 4½" x 59½"	Two 4½" x 78½"	Two 7½" x 99½"	Two 4½" x 29½"
		Border 2	Two 4½" x 48½"	Two 4½" x 67½"	Two 7½" x 113½"	Two 4½" x 28½"

We used a charm pack collection of pre-cut 5" squares to get an assortment of 24 prints for the corners.
Note: Purchase a layer cake collection of pre-cut 10" squares if making larger sizes: one layer cake for a throw, two layer cakes for a double, four layer cakes for king.

Quilt originally appeared in *10-Minute Blocks*

Cutting

Refer to the chart on page 52 for yardage and cutting.

Block, Quilt Top, and Border Assembly

1. Refer to the Basic Ten-Minute Block instructions on pages 18–19.

2. Make six blocks.

3. See How to Make Extra Centers on this page.

4. Refer to the quilt top assembly diagram to sew the blocks together.

Make six

Border 1

1. Cut three strips 1½" x width of fabric.

2. Cut two strips 1½" x 27½" for sides.

3. Cut two strips 1½" x 19½" for top and bottom.

4. Sew side borders to the quilt. Press.

5. Sew top and bottom borders to the quilt. Press.

Border 2

1. Cut 2 strips 4½" x 29½" for sides.

2. Cut 2 strips 4½" x 27½" for top and bottom.

3. Sew side borders to the quilt. Press.

4. Sew top and bottom borders to the quilt. Press.

Finishing

Quilting

Quilt as desired.

Binding

1. Cut strips 2½" wide.

2. Sew strips together end to end to equal 138".

3. Follow the binding instructions starting on page 58 or page 64.

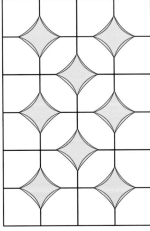

Quilt top assembly diagram

How to Make Extra Centers

1. Arrange blocks on a table in three rows, with two squares per row.

2. Number the blocks 1, 2, 3, 4, 5, and 6.

3. Pin a C folded center to the bottom left corner of Blocks 2 and 4, aligning the left and bottom raw edges.

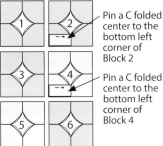

Pin a C folded center to the bottom left corner of Block 2

Pin a C folded center to the bottom left corner of Block 4

4. Place Block 1 over Block 2 with right sides together.

5. Sew along the left side. Press.

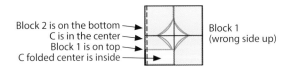

Block 2 is on the bottom
C is in the center
Block 1 is on top
C folded center is inside

Block 1 (wrong side up)

6. Open the sewn Blocks 1 and 2. Fold with wrong sides together and the C folded center sticking out as shown.

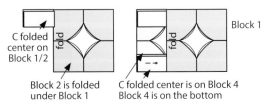

C folded center on Block 1/2

fold

Block 2 is folded under Block 1

C folded center is on Block 4
Block 4 is on the bottom

Block 1

fold

7. Turn the piece to match the diagram.

8. Lay Block 4 on a table with the right side up.

9. Align the C folded center of Blocks 1/2 with the upper left corner of Block 4.

10. Place Block 3 on top, right sides together, aligning the left raw edges.

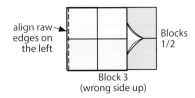

align raw edges on the left

Blocks 1/2

Block 3 (wrong side up)

11. Sew along the left side. Press.

12. Open the C folded center as before. Sew the third seam as usual.

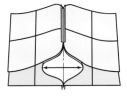

13. Repeat for the next row.

Plaid Quilt

By Choly Knight
Finished size: 36" x 48" (92 x 122cm)

The plaid effect is created by choosing colors that are blends of their neighbors to simulate the woven stripes that go through a piece of plaid fabric. Adopting a monochromatic color scheme makes creating the palette much simpler. Here is a palette example that will make selecting your fabrics much more streamlined.

Materials

- ½ yard cotton fabric in Color A
- ¾ yard cotton fabric in Color B
- ½ yard cotton fabric in Color C
- ½ yard cotton fabric in Color D
- Fat quarter cotton fabric in Color E
- Fat quarter cotton fabric in Color F
- Fat quarter cotton fabric in Color G
- 1½ yards cotton fabric for binding
- 1½ yards cotton fabric for backing
- 38" x 50" batting
- Fat quarter of appliqué fabric (optional)
- Thread to match appliqué fabric (optional)
- Fusible web (optional)
- Stabilizer (optional)
- Template plastic and monogram templates on pages 152–153.

Fabric name	Color
A	Light green
B	Medium green
C	Dark green
D	Dark pale green
E	White
F	Gray
G	Black

Quilt originally appeared in *Sew Baby*

Cut the various rectangle and square pieces from the fabric following the chart below:

Fabric color	Square name	Size to cut	Number to cut	Seam allowance
A	A1	5" x 5"	16	¼"
A	A2	5" x 2"	12	¼"
B	B1	5" x 5¾"	24	¼"
B	B2	2" x 5¾"	8	¼"
C	C	5¾" x 5¾"	8	¼"
D	D1	5" x 3½"	16	¼"
D	D2	3½" x 5¾"	12	¼"
E	E	2" x 2"	2	¼"
F	F	3½" x 2"	6	¼"
G	G	3½" x 3½"	4	¼"
Binding	Vertical	3½" x 54"	2	½"

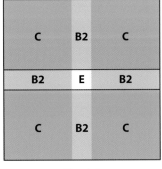

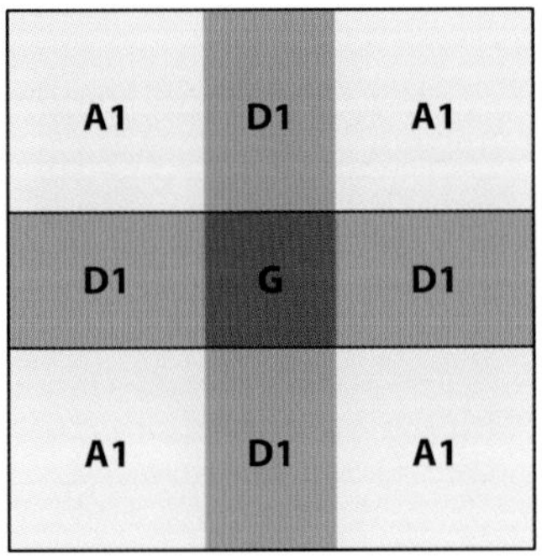

Block 1
Make four

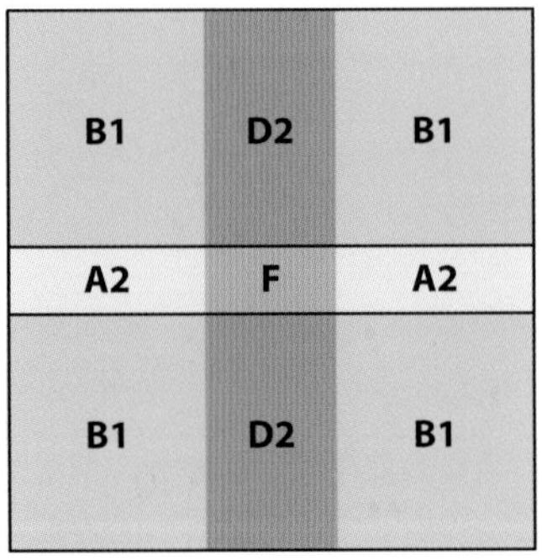

Block 2
Make six

Block 3
Make two

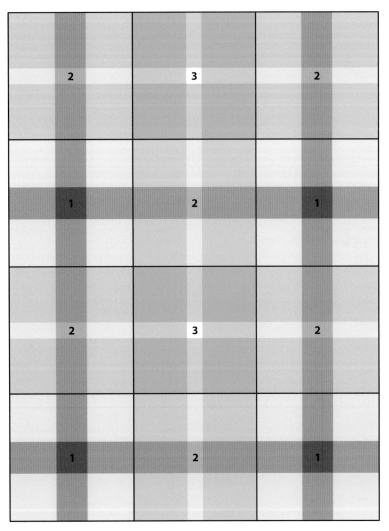

Quilt top assembly diagram

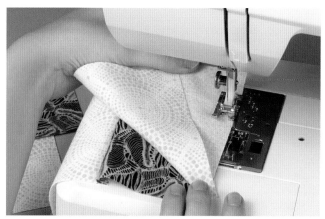

1. Cut the strips for Block 1. Use the illustration on page 55 as a guide to assemble Block 1. Sew a D1 square in between two A1 squares twice to create the top and bottom rows. Sew a G square in between two D1 squares to create the middle row.

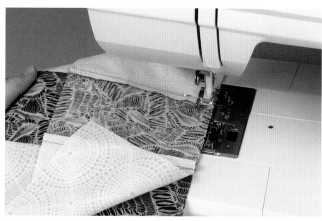

2. Sew the middle row between the top and bottom rows to finish Block 1. Repeat Steps 1–2 three more times to create four total of Block 1.

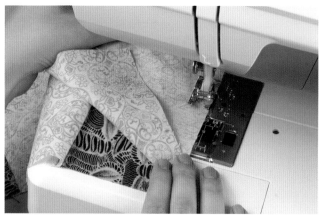

3. Cut the strips for Block 2. Use the illustration on page 55 as a guide to assemble Block 2. Sew a D2 square in between two B1 squares twice to create the top and bottom rows. Sew an F square in between two A2 squares to create the middle row.

4. Sew the middle row in between the top and bottom rows to finish Block 2. Repeat Steps 3–4 five more times to create six total of Block 2.

5. Cut the strips for Block 3. Use the illustration on page 55 as a guide to assemble Block 3. Sew a B2 square in between two C squares twice to create the top and bottom rows. Sew an E square in between two B2 squares to create the middle row.

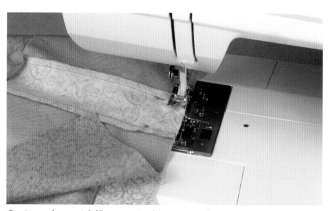

6. Sew the middle row in between the top and bottom rows to finish Block 3. Repeat Steps 5–6 once more to create two total of Block 3.

7. Sew the quilt rows. Use the illustration on page 55 as a guide to assemble the rows for the quilt top. Sew Block 3 between two of Block 2. Sew Block 2 (rotated 90°) between two of Block 1. Repeat this once more to create four rows.

8. Use the illustration on page 55 as a guide to assemble the quilt top from the rows. Sew each row to the next along the long sides, alternating them to create the quilt top.

9. Cut and apply fusible web to the appliqué fabric. Iron and sew the selected monogram letter to the bottom right corner of the quilt top, about 4" in from the edge.

10. Baste the quilt layers. Stack the backing fabric, quilt batting, and quilt top (in that order) on a large flat surface. Smooth out as many wrinkles as possible and, working outward from the middle, begin pinning the layers together with safety pins every 5"–10".

11. Quilt the layers. With a slightly longer straight stitch, sew through all the layers of the quilt along the edges of the blocks. Work from the center outward and smooth the fabric constantly, making sure all the layers are perfectly even. When it's complete, trim the excess quilt batting and backing sticking out from the quilt top.

12. Bind the edges using the instructions for squared-edge binding on pages 58–59.

Squared-Edge Binding

The squared-edge method of binding is easier for beginners, while the mitered method (see page 64) produces a more professional look but is a little more complex.

The square–edged binding style looks neat and is simple to accomplish.

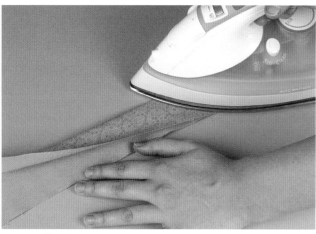

1. Iron the binding. Fold all the binding pieces in half lengthwise, wrong sides together. This will result in narrower strips of binding.

2. Sew the side binding. Pin up the side binding to the front sides of the quilt, matching raw edges. The binding should run off the end of the edges of the quilt by several inches on each side. Sew the binding to the quilt sides using a ½" seam allowance. Trim the excess binding flush with the edge of the quilt.

3. Flip the side binding over toward the back side of the quilt. Fold the binding so it wraps around the edge and iron in place.

4. Finish the side binding. From the front of the quilt, sew along the edge of the binding seam line. This should catch the other edge of the binding from the back, finishing the binding for the sides.

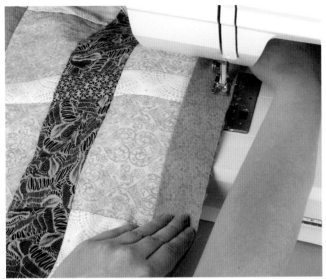

5. Pin up the top and bottom binding to the top and bottom of the quilt matching raw edges. The binding should run off the end of the edges of the quilt by several inches on each side. Sew the binding to the quilt sides using a ½" seam allowance. Iron the binding away from the quilt.

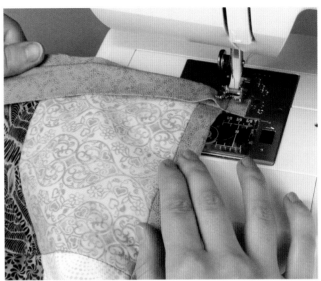

6. Sew the corners. Flip the binding back on itself and sew the edges about ⅛" away from the corner of the quilt. Trim the excess fabric.

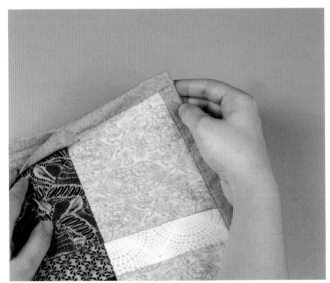

7. Turn the corners inside out and flip the binding around the edge of the quilt. The newly sewn corners should now snugly encompass the corners of the quilt. Fold the rest of the binding so it wraps around the edge similar to Step 3. Iron in place.

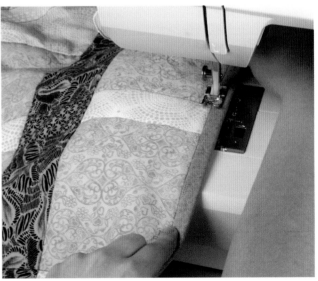

8. Finish the top and bottom. From the front of the quilt, sew along the edge of the binding seam line similar to Step 4. This should catch the other edge of the binding from the back, finishing the binding for the quilt.

Argyle Quilt

By Choly Knight
Finished size: 36¾" x 55" (94 x 140mm)

Argyle is a classic pattern that takes on many different looks depending on the color scheme; pretty pastels are sweet, while warm, autumn colors are cozy and inviting. Cool neutrals are sleek and sophisticated, while bold neon colors paired with black are funky and fun. This design also works wonderfully with the monogram appliqués from the Plaid Quilt on page 54; it's optional but will add a special touch. Either way, the look is anything but babyish, making it a keepsake you'll want to hold on to.

Materials

- 1¾ yards cotton fabric in Color A
- 1¼ yards cotton fabric in Color B
- 1¾ yards cotton fabric for binding
- 1¾ yards cotton fabric for backing
- 12 yards ⅝" ribbon
- 37" x 56" batting
- Fat quarter of appliqué fabric (optional)
- Thread to match appliqué fabric (optional)
- Fusible web (optional)
- Stabilizer (optional)
- Template plastic and monogram templates on pages 152–153 (optional)

To make the most of your quilt's color palette, be sure to choose fabrics and ribbon in light, medium, and dark shades. The color choices and order you put them in can be up to you, but the contrast in darkness will really make your fabric and ribbon pop!

Cut the various rectangle and square pieces from the fabric following the chart below:

Fabric color	Size to cut	Number to cut	Seam allowance
A	13½" x 13½"	12	¼"
B	13½" x 13½"	6	¼"
Horizontal binding	3½ " x 44"	2	½"
Vertical binding	3½" x 60"	2	½"

Quilt originally appeared in *Sew Baby*

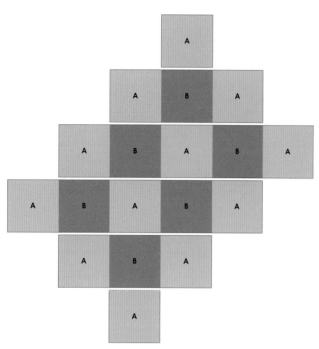

Use this illustration to correctly assemble your quilt squares into the diamond pattern.

1. Sew the block rows. Using the illustration at left as a guide, sew the rows of A and B squares. Sew one B square between two A squares twice (making two rows of three). Do the following twice: sew one A square between two B squares, then sew one more A square to each end (making two rows of five).

2. Finish the quilt top. Using the illustration as a guide, sew the rows together. Sew the five-square rows together, sew the three-square rows to the outsides, then sew the last two squares to the corners.

3. Trim the quilt top. Turn the quilt top 45° so that each square now appears as a diamond. Trim the pointed edges of the squares so that the quilt top is now an even rectangle.

4. Baste the quilt layers. Stack the backing fabric, quilt batting, and quilt top (in that order) on a large flat surface. Smooth out as many wrinkles as possible and, working outward from the middle, begin pinning the layers together with safety pins every 5"–10".

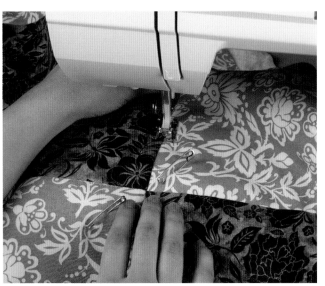

5. Quilt the layers. With a slightly longer straight stitch, sew through all the layers of the quilt along the edges of the squares. Work from the center outward and smooth the fabric constantly, making sure all the layers are perfectly even. When it's complete, trim the excess quilt batting and backing sticking out from the quilt top.

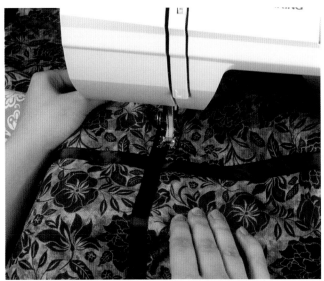

6. Pin the lengths of ribbon running down the middle of each square, going parallel to the squares' sides. Sew the ribbon down along the edges to complete the crisscrossing pattern.

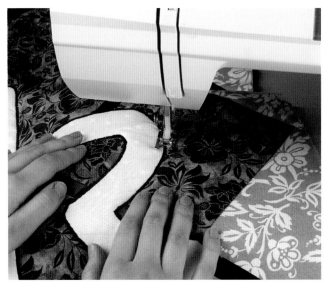

7. Appliqué the monogram. Apply fusible web to the appliqué fabric. Appliqué the selected monogram letter to the bottom right corner of the quilt top, about 4" in from the edge.

8. Bind the edges using the instructions for mitered-edge binding on pages 64-65.

Mitered-Edge Binding

The mitered-edge binding style is more complex than the squared-edged version, but it is worth the extra effort.

1. Chain all the binding pieces. Sew the four binding pieces together into a long line. Do this by sewing the the short ends together along the bias (45° to the grain)—it creates a less noticable join between the strips. Trim the excess fabric, unfold the fabric along the seam, and press it flat, which creates one long strip.

2. Iron the binding strip. Iron the entire binding strip in half, wrong sides together, to create one very long binding strip. This should be long enough to go around the edge of your quilt with about 12" or more left over.

3. Begin the mitered corner. Starting from the middle bottom edge of the quilt, line up the binding about 6" in from the strip to the edge of the quilt with raw edges together. Using a ½" seam allowance, sew the binding to the quilt edge, stopping ½" from the corner and sewing out at a 45° angle toward the corner point.

4. Fold the mitered corner. Fold the strip at a 45° angle away from the quilt then back down, creating another fold that is flush with the quilt edge. Hold these folds in place in preparation for the next step.

5. Finish the mitered corner. Starting at the very edge of the quilt with very strong backstitches, sew the other half of the corner binding to the next edge of the quilt, still keeping the ½" seam allowance. Repeat Steps 3–5 for the other corners of the quilt, and stop about 6" short of reaching the beginning point.

6. Attach the ends. Find where the binding ends meet together while remaining flush with the quilt. Open the binding up and sew the ends together with right sides facing. Fold the binding back and sew it to the quilt the same as the rest of the binding.

7. Flip the binding. Open the binding out and away from the quilt front and iron open. Wrap the binding around the edge of the quilt and iron in place. The corners in back are folded much like an envelope to achieve the mitered look.

8. Finish the binding. From the front of the quilt, sew along the seam of the binding around the perimeter of the quilt. This should catch the edge of the binding from the other side, finishing the binding.

Spotted Stars

Inspired by Lynette Jensen's Fancy Flywheels Wallhanging, recreated by Jeri Simon, quilted by E.B. Updegraff
Finished size: 34" x 34" (86 x 86cm)

This colorful design makes a cozy quilt, but it's also a suitable size to hang on the wall of a nursery or toddler's room for a cheerful, decorative touch.

Materials

- ½ yard large floral print fabric for fussy cut block centers
- ¼ yard white print fabric for blocks
- ¼ yard orange multi-dot fabric for blocks
- ½ yard light blue fabric for blocks
- ⅓ yard white multi-dot fabric for blocks and lattice post squares
- ½ yard teal fabric for lattice segments
- ⅓ yard striped binding fabric
- 1¼ yards backing fabric
- 40" square batting

Fabric quantities based on 42"–44"-wide 100% cotton fabrics.
WOF = width of fabric
Sew with a ¼" seam allowance unless otherwise stated.

Cutting

From the large floral print fabric, fussy cut:
- Four 3½" squares

Note: I centered a flower in each square.

From the white print fabric, cut:
- Three 2" x WOF strips. From the strips, subcut:
  - Eight 2" x 3½" rectangles
  - Eight 2" x 6½" rectangles

From the orange multi-dot fabric, cut:
- One 3⅞" x WOF strip

From the light blue fabric, cut:
- One 3⅞" x WOF strip
- Two 3½" x WOF strips. From the strips, subcut:
  - Sixteen 3½" squares

From the white multi-dot fabric, cut:
- Three 3½" x WOF strips. From two strips, subcut:
  - Sixteen 3½" squares
- From the remaining strip, subcut:
  - Nine 3½" lattice post squares

From the teal fabric, cut:
- Four 3½" x WOF strips. From the strips, subcut:
  - Twelve 3½" x 12½" lattice segments

From the striped fabric, cut:
- Four 2½" x WOF strips for binding

Quilt originally appeared in *Simply Stars*

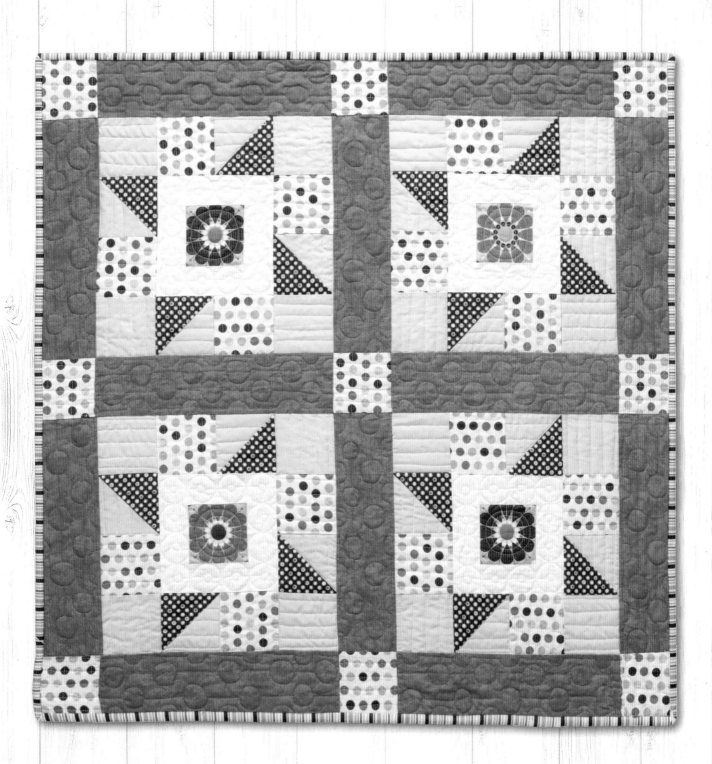

Making the Blocks

1. With right sides together, sew 2" x 3½" white print rectangles to opposite sides of a 3½" large floral print square. Press.

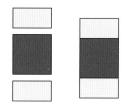

2. With right sides together, sew 2" x 6½" white print rectangles to the remaining sides of the large floral print square in Step 1. Press to make a 6½" block center. Make four block centers.

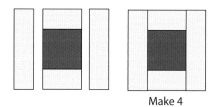

Make 4

3. With right sides together, layer the 3⅞" x WOF orange multi-dot print and light blue strips together. Press. Cut the layered strips into 3⅞" squares. Cut the squares in half diagonally to make sixteen sets of triangles.

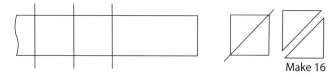

Make 16

4. Stitch ¼" from the long edge of each set of triangles. Press the triangles open to make sixteen 3½" half-square triangles.

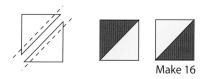

Make 16

5. Sew a 3½" white multi-dot square to the left edge of each half-square triangle as shown. Press. Make sixteen units.

Make 16

6. Referring to the diagram, sew a unit to the top and bottom edges of each block center. Press.

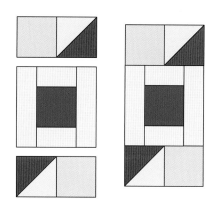

7. Sew 3½" light blue squares to the ends of the remaining Step 5 units. Press.

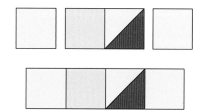

8. Sew the Step 7 units to the remaining sides of the block center. Press to make a block. Make four 12½" blocks.

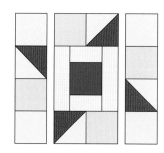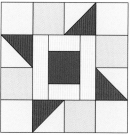

Make 4

Quilt Top Assembly

1. Lay out three 3½" x 12½" teal lattice segments and two blocks in a row as shown. Sew the pieces together to make a block row. Press the seam allowances toward the lattice segments. Make two block rows.

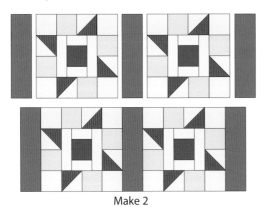

Make 2

2. Lay out two 3½" x 12½" teal lattice segments and three 3½" white multi-dot lattice post squares in a row as shown. Sew the pieces together to make a sashing row. Press the seam allowances toward the lattice segments. Make three sashing rows.

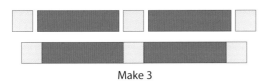

Make 3

3. Referring to the assembly diagram, lay out the block and sashing rows as shown.

Quilt top assembly diagram

4. Sew the rows together, pinning at the seam intersections as needed. Press the seam allowances in one direction.

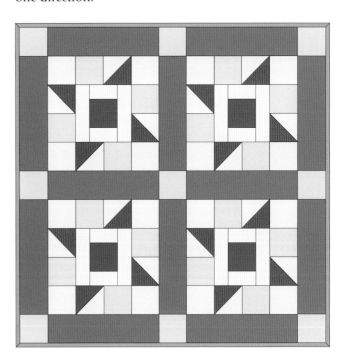

Finishing

1. Layer the backing, batting, and quilt top. Quilt as desired.

2. Sew the binding strips together to make one continuous strip. Press the strip in half, wrong sides together, along the length. Sew the binding to the edges of the quilt. Turn the binding over the edge to the back of the quilt and stitch in place.

Irish Chain Sandman

By Carol C. Porter and Rebecca J. Hansen
Finished size: 35½" x 43¼" (90 x 110cm)

Calling to mind the warm sand and gentle waves, these Irish Chain blocks in beachy neutrals with a pop of blue will lull baby into dreamland.

Materials

- ½ yard background fabric
- ¼ yard Fabric 1, light print
- ¼ yard Fabric 2, light/ medium print
- ⅓ yard Fabric 3, medium print
- ⅓ yard Fabric 4, light/dark print
- ⅓ yard Fabric 5, dark print
- ⅓ yard Fabric 6, light/dark print
- ⅓ yard Fabric 7, medium print
- ⅓ yard Fabric 8, light/ medium print
- ⅓ yard Fabric 9, light print
- ¼ yard Border 1
- ⅛ yard Border 2
- ⅜ yard Border 3
- 1¼ yards backing fabric
- ⅓ yard fabric for binding
- Batting

Cutting

From the background fabric:
- Cut two 1½"-wide strips, selvage to selvage. Then subcut the two strips into thirty-one 1½" x 1½" squares total.
- Cut three 1½"-wide strips, selvage to selvage. Then subcut the three strips into twenty-four 1½" x 3½" rectangles.
- Cut one 5½"-wide strip, selvage to selvage. Then subcut the strip into six 5½" x 5½" squares.

From Fabrics 1–9:
- Cut the following strips from selvage to selvage, each 1½" wide. Place the fabric number on the stack of strips for easy identification when it comes time to sew the strips together.
  - Fabric 1: Cut three strips
  - Fabric 2: Cut four strips
  - Fabric 3: Cut four strips
  - Fabric 4: Cut five strips
  - Fabric 5: Cut five strips
  - Fabric 6: Cut five strips
  - Fabric 7: Cut five strips
  - Fabric 8: Cut four strips
  - Fabric 9: Cut four strips

Follow the chart at right to cut the necessary strata units.

Block and Quilt Top Assembly

Refer to the diagrams on pages 72 and 73 to put the blocks together and then assemble the quilt top.

Quilt originally appeared in *Seaside Quilts*

Adding the Borders

1. From Border Fabric 1, cut four 1½"-wide strips.

2. From Border Fabric 2, cut four ¾"-wide strips.

3. From Border Fabric 3, cut four 2½"-wide strips.

4. Sew the side borders to the quilt top first, and then sew the top and bottom borders to the quilt top in order.

Finishing

1. Mark the quilt top with a design of your choice.

2. Layer the quilt top with the batting and backing; baste it in place.

3. Quilt as desired, then bind the edges; follow the binding instructions starting on page 58 or page 64.

4. Add a label, then sign, date, and photograph your finished quilt.

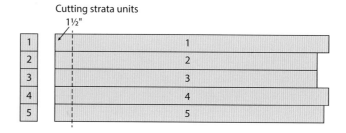
Cutting strata units

Block assembly diagram

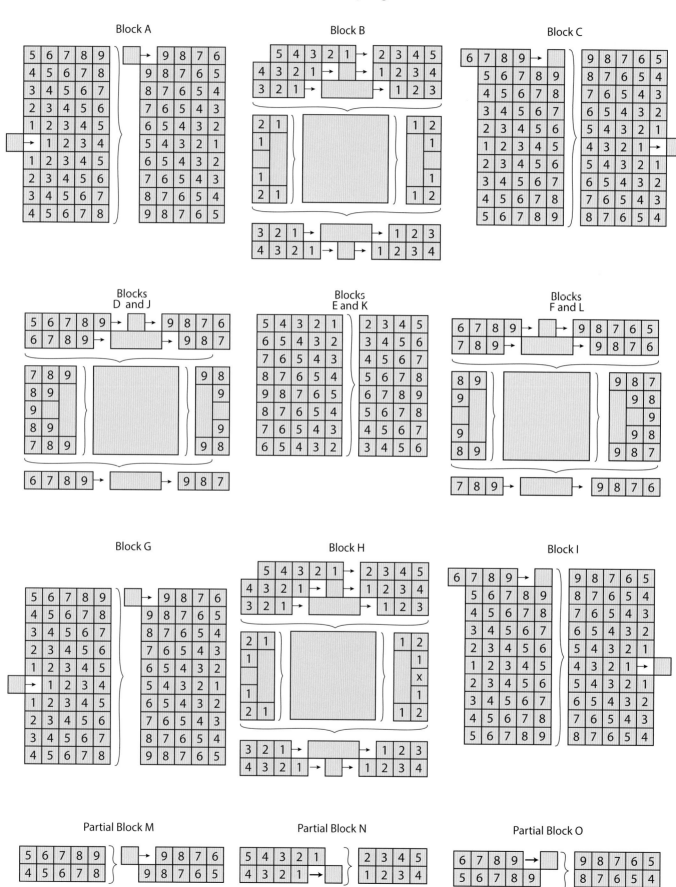

Quilt top assembly diagram

Block A

```
5 6 7 8 9   9 8 7 6
4 5 6 7 8 9 8 7 6 5
3 4 5 6 7 8 7 6 5 4
2 3 4 5 6 7 6 5 4 3
1 2 3 4 5 6 5 4 3 2
  1 2 3 4 5 4 3 2 1
1 2 3 4 5 6 5 4 3 2
2 3 4 5 6 7 6 5 4 3
3 4 5 6 7 8 7 6 5 4
4 5 6 7 8 9 8 7 6 5
```

Block B

```
5 4 3 2 1   2 3 4 5
4 3 2 1     1 2 3 4
3 2 1       1 2 3
2 1         1 2
1               1
              x
1               1
2 1         1 2
3 2 1       1 2 3
4 3 2 1   1 2 3 4
```

Block C

```
6 7 8 9   9 8 7 6 5
5 6 7 8 9 8 7 6 5 4
4 5 6 7 8 7 6 5 4 3
3 4 5 6 7 6 5 4 3 2
2 3 4 5 6 5 4 3 2 1
1 2 3 4 5 4 3 2 1
2 3 4 5 6 5 4 3 2 1
3 4 5 6 7 6 5 4 3 2
4 5 6 7 8 7 6 5 4 3
5 6 7 8 9 8 7 6 5 4
```

Block D

```
5 6 7 8 9   9 8 7 6
6 7 8 9       9 8 7
7 8 9         9 8
8 9             9
9
8 9             9
7 8 9         9 8
6 7 8 9     9 8 7
```

Block E

```
5 4 3 2 1 2 3 4 5
6 5 4 3 2 3 4 5 6
7 6 5 4 3 4 5 6 7
8 7 6 5 4 5 6 7 8
9 8 7 6 5 6 7 8 9
8 7 6 5 4 5 6 7 8
7 6 5 4 3 4 5 6 7
6 5 4 3 2 3 4 5 6
```

Block F

```
6 7 8 9   9 8 7 6 5
7 8 9       9 8 7 6
8 9           9 8 7
9               9 8
                  9
9               9 8
8 9           9 8 7
7 8 9       9 8 7 6
```

Block G

```
5 6 7 8 9   9 8 7 6
4 5 6 7 8 9 8 7 6 5
3 4 5 6 7 8 7 6 5 4
2 3 4 5 6 7 6 5 4 3
1 2 3 4 5 6 5 4 3 2
  1 2 3 4 5 4 3 2 1
1 2 3 4 5 6 5 4 3 2
2 3 4 5 6 7 6 5 4 3
3 4 5 6 7 8 7 6 5 4
4 5 6 7 8 9 8 7 6 5
```

Block H

```
5 4 3 2 1   2 3 4 5
4 3 2 1     1 2 3 4
3 2 1       1 2 3
2 1         1 2
1               1
              x
1               1
2 1         1 2
3 2 1       1 2 3
4 3 2 1   1 2 3 4
```

Block I

```
6 7 8 9   9 8 7 6 5
5 6 7 8 9 8 7 6 5 4
4 5 6 7 8 7 6 5 4 3
3 4 5 6 7 6 5 4 3 2
2 3 4 5 6 5 4 3 2 1
1 2 3 4 5 4 3 2 1
2 3 4 5 6 5 4 3 2 1
3 4 5 6 7 6 5 4 3 2
4 5 6 7 8 7 6 5 4 3
5 6 7 8 9 8 7 6 5 4
```

Block J

```
5 6 7 8 9   9 8 7 6
6 7 8 9       9 8 7
7 8 9         9 8
8 9             9
9
8 9             9
7 8 9         9 8
6 7 8 9     9 8 7
```

Block K

```
5 4 3 2 1 2 3 4 5
6 5 4 3 2 3 4 5 6
7 6 5 4 3 4 5 6 7
8 7 6 5 4 5 6 7 8
9 8 7 6 5 6 7 8 9
8 7 6 5 4 5 6 7 8
7 6 5 4 3 4 5 6 7
6 5 4 3 2 3 4 5 6
```

Block L

```
6 7 8 9   9 8 7 6 5
7 8 9       9 8 7 6
8 9           9 8 7
9               9 8
                  9
9               9 8
8 9           9 8 7
7 8 9       9 8 7 6
```

Partial Block M

```
5 6 7 8 9   9 8 7 6
4 5 6 7 8 9 8 7 6 5
```

Partial Block N

```
5 4 3 2 1 2 3 4 5
4 3 2 1   1 2 3 4
```

Partial Block O

```
6 7 8 9   9 8 7 6 5
5 6 7 8 9 8 7 6 5 4
```

Jeweled Lattice

By Choly Knight
Finished size: 37½" x 55½" (95 x 141cm)

This quilt is a scrap lover's delight! With loads of tiny pieces surrounded by a bright and fresh lattice border, all of your little fabric scraps will look amazing together. The construction of the quilt is also loads of fun. Not only is it simple, but variety abounds because you can switch and swap out blocks as you go.

Materials

- ½ yard violet fabric
- ½ yard teal fabric
- ¼ yard seafoam fabric
- ¼ yard orange fabric
- ¼ yard magenta fabric
- 1¼ yards border fabric
- 45" x 63" batting
- 1⅔ yards x 45" backing fabric
- ½ yard binding fabric

WOF = width of fabric

Pre-cut Perfect!

The pattern for this project works perfectly with pre-cut strip sets such as jelly rolls. Use them as the focus fabrics to make all the squares—it helps to cut more squares than you need so you're sure that the right fabrics match up. You can always use extras to piece the back! For this baby quilt, get a bundle with at least nineteen strips to have enough focus fabric. For the twin size, you'll need thirty-four strips; for full, forty-three; for queen, fifty-five; and at least sixty-seven for a king.

Cutting

Gather all of the patchwork fabrics for now; set aside all of the backing fabrics and batting for later. Cut your fabric strips across the width of the fabric yardage. Make any subcuts as instructed, then sort and pile your fabrics separated by letter and color, labeling with a sticky note as necessary.

From the teal and violet fabrics, cut:
- Five strips from each color: 2½" x WOF (ten total). From the strips, subcut:
  - Eighteen rectangles from each color: 3½" x 2½" (thirty-six total) (A)
  - Eighteen rectangles from each color: 5½" x 2½" (thirty-six total) (B)

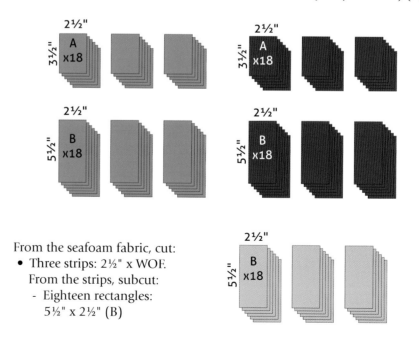

From the seafoam fabric, cut:
- Three strips: 2½" x WOF. From the strips, subcut:
  - Eighteen rectangles: 5½" x 2½" (B)

Quilt originally appeared in *Quilting Simplified*

From the orange and magenta fabrics, cut:
- Three strips from each color: 2½" x WOF (six total). From the strips, subcut:
  - Thirty-six squares from each color: 2½" x 2½" (72 total) (C)

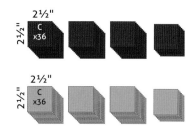

- Twenty-nine strips: 1½" x WOF. From the strips, subcut:
  - Seventy-two rectangles: 2½" x 1½" (D)
  - Eighteen rectangles: 3½" x 1½" (E)
  - Thirty-six rectangles: 5½" x 1½" (F)
  - Eighteen rectangles: 6½" x 1½" (G)
  - Twenty-one strips: 17½" x 1½" (H)
  - Four strips: 37½" x 1½" (I)

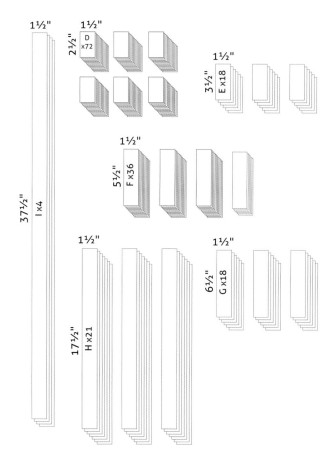

Piecing and Quilt Top Assembly

Use a scant ¼" (6mm) seam allowance for all seams. Press seam allowances open or to the side as desired.

1. The quilt blocks are made from three units, sewn with sashing in between. Referring to Fig. A, construct Unit 1 as follows.
- Sew a C square to a D rectangle.
- Then add an E rectangle (in the same color as D) on top.
- Next, sew an A rectangle to the left.
- And finally, sew a B rectangle (in the same color as A) to the top.

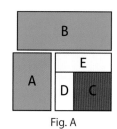

Fig. A

2. Construct Unit 2 as described below, following along with Fig. B.
- Sew a C square to a D rectangle.
- Then add an A rectangle to the bottom. We'll call this one side. Set it aside for the time being.
- Sew a B rectangle (shown in seafoam in the illustration) to a D rectangle, making another side.
- Attach the two sides with a G rectangle in between.
- Add a B rectangle (in the same color as A) to the bottom.

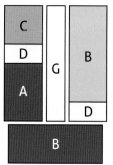

Fig. B

3. Construct Unit 3 by sewing a D rectangle between two C squares (Fig. C).

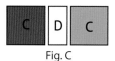

Fig. C

4. Here comes the fun part, where you finish the column. Arrange the three units you've made however you like in a column, putting them in whatever order or placement that suits you, and then sew them with F rectangles in between (Fig. D).

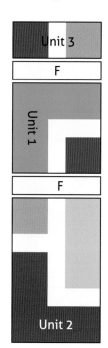

Fig. D

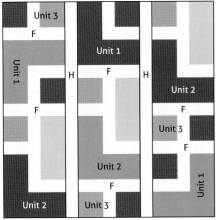

Fig. E

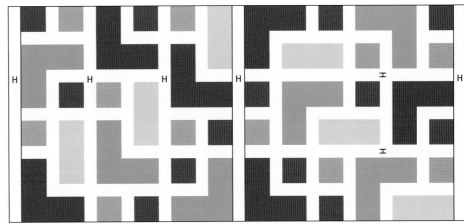

Fig. F

Fig. G (Quilt top assembly diagram)

5. Repeat Steps 1–4 twice more to create three columns. Join the columns into a square block by sewing them together with H rectangles in between (Fig. E). Repeat Steps 1–5 five more times to create six blocks total.

6. Create a row by joining two blocks together with an H strip between them, and attach an H strip on each end (Fig. F). Repeat this twice more to create three rows.

7. Join all three rows together with the I strips between them and on the top and bottom (Fig. G).

Finishing

Layer the backing, batting, and quilt top. Baste the layers and quilt as desired, then bind the raw edges. Follow the binding instructions starting on page 58 or page 64.

Quilt It!

This quilt has quite a lot going on with all its tiny pieces, so I kept the quilting basic with some crisscrossing diagonal lines. To make things super easy, I marked the lines with masking tape and used a walking foot. The resulting diamond pattern goes along with the "jewel" theme and also introduces just a bit of contrast to the whole piece.

Just My Size: Jeweled Lattice Baby Quilt

Instead of a baby quilt, would you like to make something bigger? Simply repeat more blocks to get the size that you need. Refer to the layout and chart for the sizes and proper quantities, and create the quilt as described in the instructions.

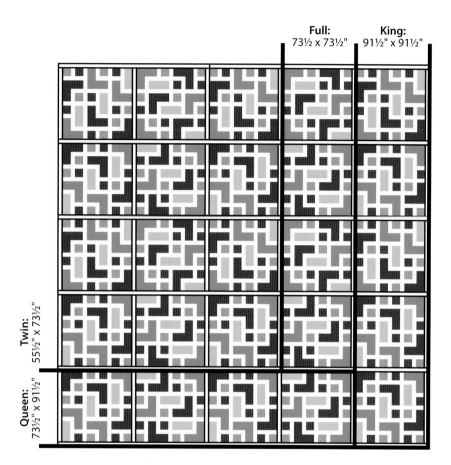

Full: 73½ x 73½"

King: 91½" x 91½"

Twin: 55½" x 73½"

Queen: 73½" x 91½"

Quilt layout: Use the number of blocks indicated by the illustration and the chart to construct your quilt to size.

Color variations

Would you like to make this quilt in a different color palette? Check out the options here to spark your creativity.

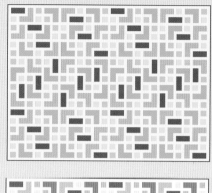

	Twin	Full	Queen	King
Finished size	55½" x 73½"	73½" x 73½"	73½" x 91½"	91½" x 91½"
Block configuration	3 blocks x 4 rows (12 total)	4 blocks x 4 rows (16 total)	4 blocks x 5 rows (20 total)	5 blocks x 5 rows (25 total)
Materials needed				
Violet and teal fabrics, each:	⅔ yard	1 yard	1¼ yards	1⅓ yards
Seafoam fabric	½ yard	½ yard	⅔ yard	1 yard
Orange and magenta fabrics, each:	½ yard	½ yard	⅔ yard	¾ yard
Border fabric	2½ yards	3¼ yards	4 yards	5 yards
Batting	64" x 82"	82" x 82"	82" x 100"	100" x 100"
Backing	2 yards of 106"-wide backing	2½ yards of 106"-wide backing	2½ yards of 106"-wide backing	3 yards of 106"-wide backing
Binding	⅔ yard	¾ yard	¾ yard	1 yard
Violet/teal fabrics				
Strips to cut of each:	9 strips: 2½" x WOF	12 strips: 2½" x WOF	15 strips: 2½" x WOF	18 strips: 2½" x WOF
Subcut into:	36 rectangles: 3½" x 2½" (A)	48 rectangles: 3½" x 2½" (A)	60 rectangles: 3½" x 2½" (A)	75 rectangles: 3½" x 2½" (A)
	36 rectangles: 5½" x 2½" (B)	48 rectangles: 5½" x 2½" (B)	60 rectangles: 5½" x 2½" (B)	75 rectangles: 5½" x 2½" (B)
Seafoam fabric				
Strips to cut:	6 strips: 2½" (6.4cm) x WOF	7 strips: 2½" (6.4cm) x WOF	9 strips: 2½" (6.4cm) x WOF	11 strips: 2½" (6.4cm) x WOF
Subcut into:	36 rectangles: 5½" x 2½" (B)	48 rectangles: 5½" x 2½" (B)	60 rectangles: 5½" x 2½" (B)	75 rectangles: 5½" x 2½" (B)
Orange/magenta fabrics				
Strips to cut of each:	5 strips: 2½" x WOF	6 strips: 2½" x WOF	8 strips: 2½" x WOF	10 strips: 2½" x WOF
Subcut into:	72 squares: 2½" x 2½" (C)	96 squares: 2½" x 2½" (C)	120 squares: 2½" x 2½" (C)	150 squares: 2½" x 2½" (C)
Border fabric				
Strips to cut:	59 strips: 1½ x WOF	74 strips: 1½ x WOF	95 strips: 1½ x WOF	114 strips: 1½ x WOF
Horizontal sashing:	Chain 8 strips, then subcut into 5 strips: 55½" x 1½" (I)	Chain 10 strips, then subcut into 5 strips: 73½" x 1½" (I)	Chain 12 strips, then subcut into 6 strips: 73½" x 1½" (I)	Chain 15 strips, then subcut into 6 strips: 91½" x 1½" (I)
Working from the longest to the shortest to use the strips most efficiently, subcut into:	144 rectangles 2½" x 1½" (D)	192 rectangles 2½" x 1½" (D)	240 rectangles 2½" x 1½" (D)	300 rectangles 2½" x 1½" (D)
	36 rectangles 3½" x 1½" (E)	48 rectangles 3½" x 1½" (E)	60 rectangles 3½" x 1½" (E)	75 rectangles 3½" x 1½" (E)
	72 rectangles 5½" x 1½" (F)	96 rectangles 5½" x 1½" (F)	120 rectangles 5½" x 1½" (F)	150 rectangles 5½" x 1½" (F)
	36 rectangles 6½" x 1½" (G)	48 rectangles 6½" x 1½" (G)	60 rectangles 6½" x 1½" (G)	75 rectangles 6½" x 1½" (G)
	40 rectangles 17½" x 1½" (H)	52 rectangles 17½" x 1½" (H)	65 rectangles 17½" x 1½" (H)	80 rectangles 17½" x 1½" (H)

Part 2

FLOOR QUILTS

Selvage Pinwheels

By Mary M. Hogan
Finished size: Approximately 52" x 52" (132 x 132cm)

Selvage strings create stripes when sewn into blocks. The Selvage Pinwheels quilt uses selvages that are at least 1½" wide. The blocks go together quickly due to a solid triangle covering one side of each foundation square. When the blocks are sewn together in groups of four, they form pinwheels. Regular fabric strings can be used instead of selvages if desired.

Materials

- Sixty-four 6½" square foundations
- Assorted 1½" selvage strings for blocks
- 1⅔ yards teal fabric for blocks and borders
- ½ yard green fabric for blocks
- ½ yard binding fabric
- 2⅞ yards backing fabric
- Batting

Note: Fabric requirements may vary depending on the width and placement of strings.

WOF = width of fabric
Fabric is 42"–44" wide unless otherwise noted.

Design Elements	
Unifying elements	• Blue and green large triangles • Selvage strips
Focal point	• Green triangles in center of quilt
Variation	• Many different selvage fabrics
Color	• Dark value triangles • Light value selvages
Line and shape	• Pinwheel blocks • Lines (stripes) produced by selvages

Cutting

Note: The half-square triangles are oversized and will be trimmed after blocks are complete.

From the teal fabric, cut:
- Five 7¼" x WOF strips. From the strips, subcut:
  - Twenty-four 7¼" squares. Cut each square in half diagonally to make a total of forty-eight half-square triangles.
- Eight 2½" x WOF border strips

From the green fabric, cut:
- Two 7¼" x WOF strips. From the strips, subcut:
  - Eight 7¼" squares. Cut each square in half diagonally to make a total of sixteen half-square triangles.

From the backing fabric, cut:
- One 60" x WOF piece
- Two 21" x WOF pieces

From the binding fabric, cut:
- Six 2½" x WOF strips

Making the Blocks

1. Draw a diagonal line ¼" from the center of a foundation square.

2. Place a teal half-square triangle right side up on a foundation square, matching the right raw edge of the triangle on the drawn line. Secure with pins if desired.

Quilt originally appeared in *String Quilt Style*

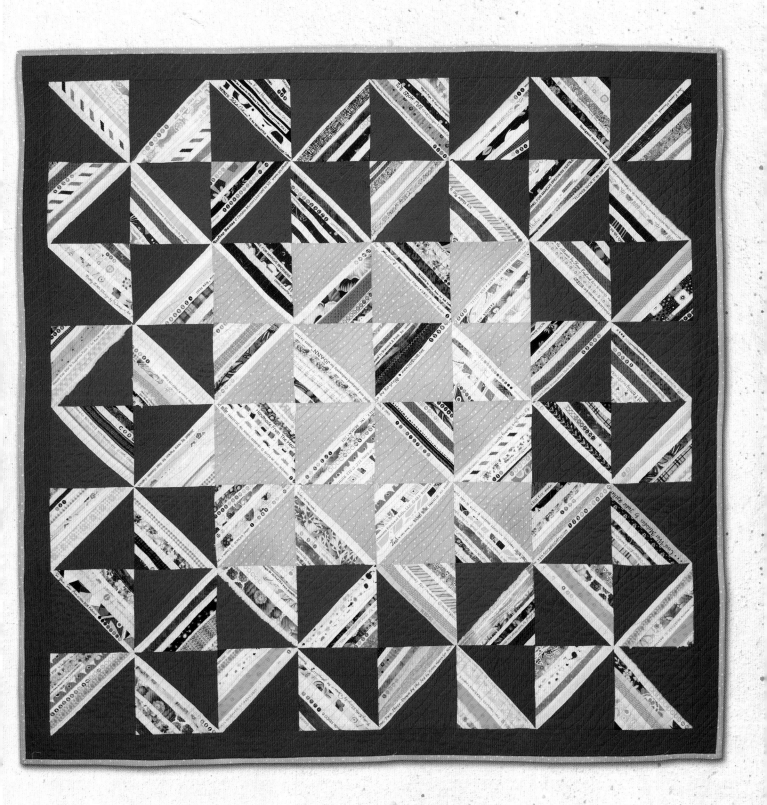

3. Place a selvage string right side up on the triangle, overlapping it approximately ¼". Pin the selvage in place. Sew the selvage in place using a zigzag stitch to cover the edge of the selvage. Press.

Note: If using a straight stitch, stitch right at the finished edge of the selvage.

4. To complete the block, continue adding selvages until the foundation is covered. Make a total of forty-eight teal blocks.

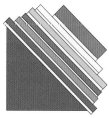

Make
forty-eight

5. Referring to Steps 1–4, make a total of sixteen green blocks.

Make
sixteen

Quilt Center Assembly

1. Press blocks carefully, using starch if needed to stabilize the blocks.

2. Trim blocks to 6-½" square.

3. Remove the foundation papers.

4. Sew the selvage string blocks together in sixteen sets of four. Pay close attention to the orientation of the blocks. Make twelve teal block sets and four green block sets.

Note: When sewing diagonally pieced blocks together, use a ¼" seam allowance. Press seams open.

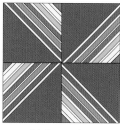 

Make twelve
sets

Make four
sets

5. Referring to the quilt center assembly diagram, lay out the block sets in four rows with four block sets in each row.

6. Sew the block sets together in rows. Press seams open.

7. Sew the rows together to complete the quilt center.

An extra block sewn to the back of the quilt makes the perfect label.

Adding the Borders

1. Sew the 2½" border strips together end to end in pairs to make four border strips.

2. Measure the quilt center from side to side and cut two border strips to this size. Sew the strips to the top and bottom of the quilt center. Press seams toward the border.

3. Measure the quilt center from top to bottom and cut two border strips to this size. Sew the strips to opposite sides of the quilt center. Press seams toward the border to complete the quilt top.

Finishing

1. Sew the two 21" x WOF backing pieces together end to end to make a 21" x 84" piece.

2. Sew the 60" x WOF backing piece to the 21" x 84" section as shown. Press seams open.

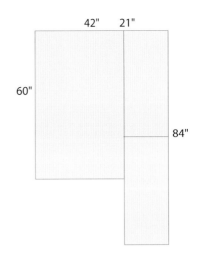

3. Trim away any excess length.

4. Layer the backing, batting and quilt top together and baste. Quilt as desired.

5. Sew the binding strips together using diagonal seams to create one continuous strip. Press the strip in half lengthwise, wrong sides together, and sew to the raw edge of the quilt top. Fold binding over raw edges and hand stitch in place.

Quilt center assembly diagram

Kids Will Be Kids

By Lynette Jensen
Finished size: 48" x 56"
(122 x 142cm)

With lots of squares, triangles, and primary colors, this traditional-looking yet playful design makes a perfect first quilt for a little one.

Materials

- ⅞ yard yellow print for blocks, narrow middle border, and wide middle border
- ⅓ yard blue print for blocks and inner border
- ⅝ yard red print for blocks and checkerboard borders
- ⅔ yard beige print for side/corner triangles and checkerboard borders
- 1 yard green print for outer border
- ⅝ yard red print for binding
- 3 yards for backing
- Batting, at least 54" x 62"

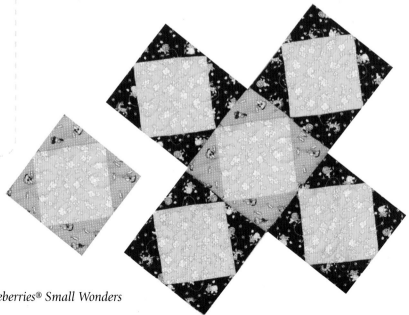

Quilt originally appeared in *Thimbleberries® Small Wonders*

Making the Blocks

Makes two blue and yellow blocks
Makes six red and yellow blocks

Cutting

From the yellow print, cut:
- One 4½" x 44" strip. From strip, subcut: eight 4½" squares

From the blue print, cut:
- One 3⅝" x 44" strip. From the strip, subcut: four 3⅝" squares. Cut the squares in half diagonally to make eight triangles.

From the red print, cut:
- Two 3⅝" x 44" strips. From the strips, subcut: twelve 3⅝" squares. Cut the squares in half diagonally to make twenty-four triangles.

3⅝" squares   3⅝" squares

Piecing

Refer to arrows on diagrams for pressing.

Note: Mark centerpoints along the side edges of each 4½" yellow square. Carefully mark the centerpoints along the bias edge of each blue and red triangle. Be careful not to stretch the bias edges.

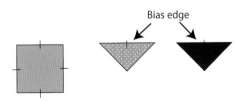

Bias edge

1. With right sides together and raw edges even, center a blue triangle at the top edge of a 4½" yellow square. Pin the layers together, being careful not to stretch the bias edges; stitch and press. In the same manner, stitch a blue triangle to the bottom edge of the yellow square; press. Stitch blue triangles to the remaining side edges of the square; press. At this point, each pieced block should measure 6⅛" square.

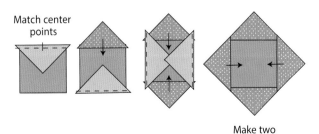

Match center points

Make two

2. With right sides together, center, pin, and stitch a red triangle to the top edge of a 4½" yellow square; press. In the same manner, stitch a red triangle to the bottom edge of the yellow square; press. Stitch the red triangles to the remaining side edges of the square; press. At this point, each pieced block should measure 6⅛" square.

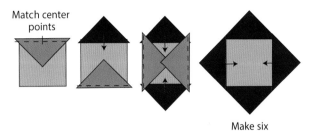

Match center points

Make six

Making the Quilt Center

Note: Side and corner triangles are larger than necessary and will be trimmed before borders are added.

Cutting

From beige print, cut:
- One 9½" x 44" strip. From the strip, subcut: two 9½" squares. Cut squares diagonally into quarters for a total of eight triangles.

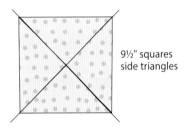

9½" squares side triangles

- Two 5½" squares. Cut the squares in half diagonally for a total of four corner triangles.

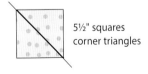

5½" squares corner triangles

Assembly

1. Referring to the quilt center assembly diagram for block placement, sew the pieced blocks, beige side triangles, and beige corner triangles together in diagonal rows. Press the seam allowances in alternating directions by rows so the seams will fit snugly together with less bulk.

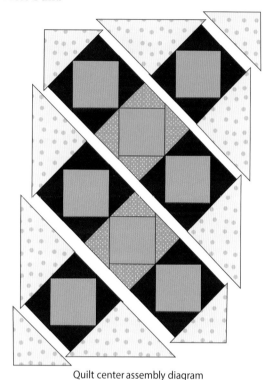

Quilt center assembly diagram

2. Trim away excess fabric from the side/corner triangles, taking care to allow a ¼" seam allowance beyond the corners of each block. Refer to Trimming Side and Corner Triangles for complete instructions. At this point, the quilt center should measure 16½ x 24½ inches.

Trimming the Side and Corner Triangles

Begin at a corner by lining up your ruler ¼" inch beyond the points of the block corners as shown. Cut along the edge of the ruler. Repeat this procedure on all four sides of the quilt top.

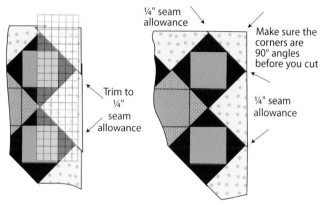

Adding the Borders

Note: Thee yardage given allows for ther border strips to be cut on the crosswise grain. Diagonally piece strips as needed.

Cutting

From the blue print, cut:
- Three 1½" x 44" inner border strips

From the yellow print, cut:
- Four 4½" x 44" wide middle border strips
- Three 1½" x 44" narrow middle border strips

From the red print, cut:
- Four 2½" x 44" strips

From the beige print, cut:
- Four 2½" x 44" strips

From the green print, cut:
- Five 6½" x 44" outer border strips

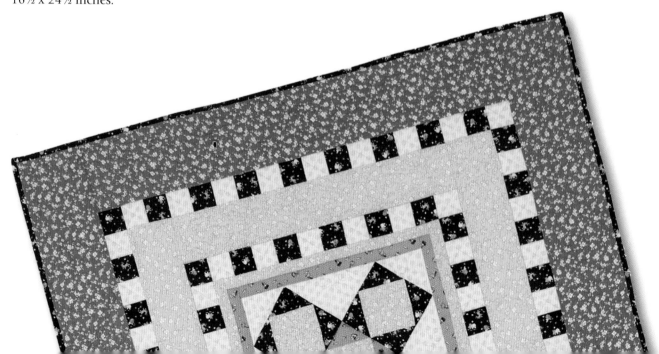

Piecing

Press the seam allowances toward the borders just added.

1. Attach the 1½"-wide blue inner border strips.

2. Attach 1½"-wide yellow narrow middle border strips.

3. Aligning the long edges, sew 2½" x 44" red and beige strips together in pairs. Press the seam allowances toward the darker fabric. Make a total of four strip sets. Cut the strip sets into segments.

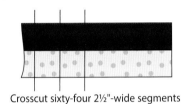

Crosscut sixty-four 2½"-wide segments

4. For the top/bottom checkerboard borders, sew five segments together; press. Sew the borders to the top/bottom edges of the quilt center; press.

Make two for top/bottom borders

5. For the side checkerboard borders, sew eight segments together; press. Sew the borders to the side edges of the quilt center; press.

Make two for side borders

6. Attach the 4½"-wide yellow middle border strips.

7. For the top/bottom checkerboard borders, sew eight segments together; press. Sew the borders to the top/bottom edges of the quilt center; press.

Make two for top/bottom borders

8. For side checkerboard borders, sew eleven segments together; press. Sew the borders to the side edges of the quilt center; press.

Make two for side borders

9. Attach 6½"-wide green outer border strips.

Putting It All Together

Cut a 3-yard length of backing fabric in half crosswise to make two 1½-yard lengths. Quilt as desired.

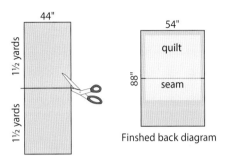

Finshed back diagram

Binding

Cutting

From the red print, cut:
- Six 2¾" x 44" strips

Sew the binding to the quilt using a ⅜" seam allowance. This measurement will produce a ½"-wide finished double binding. Refer to the binding instructions starting on page 58 or page 64.

Confetti Stars

By Lynette Jensen
Finished size: 68" x 79" (173 x 201cm)

Nothing is more traditional than the Eight-Pointed-Star quilt block. It is a staple in our quiltmaking history. This version uses a variety of fat quarter prints that are all tied together with a multi-colored floral border.

Materials

- Eight fat quarters (18" x 20" pieces) medium/dark prints for star blocks
- Eight fat quarters (18" x 20" pieces) light prints for star backgrounds
- Five fat quarters (18" x 20" pieces) medium/dark prints for alternate blocks
- Nine fat quarters (18" x 20" pieces) medium/dark prints for side/corner triangles
- 1⅔ yards large floral print for border
- ⅔ yard diagonal print for binding
- 5 yards backing fabric
- Batting, at least 76" x 87"

Note: Press seams in the directions indicated by the arrows on the diagrams. If no direction is specified, press the seams toward the darker fabric.

Quilt originally appeared in *Thimbleberries® Quilts with a New Attitude*

Making the Star Blocks

Makes thirty blocks

Cutting

From each of eight medium/dark print fat quarters, cut:
- Four 4½" squares
- Four 2½" x 20" strips. From the strips, subcut:
  - Thirty-two 2½" squares

From each of eight light print fat quarters, cut:
- Six 2½" x 20" strips. From the strips, subcut:
  - Sixteen 2½" x 4½" rectangles
  - Sixteen 2½" squares

Piecing

1. Use a pencil to draw a diagonal line on the 2½' medium/dark print squares.

2. Position the marked medium/dark print square on the corner of the 2½" x 4½" light print rectangle. Stitch on the line, trim the seam allowance to ¼", and press. Repeat this process at the opposite corner of the rectangle.

Make sixteen from each fat quarter

3. Sew the coordinating Step 2 units to the top/ bottom of the 4½" coordinating squares; press. Sew the 2½" light print squares to both sides of the remaining Step 2 units; press. Sew the units to the sides of the coordinating blocks; press. At this point, each block should measure 8½" square. You will be using thirty blocks.

Make four from each fat quarter

Quilt Center

Note: The side and corner triangles are larger than necessary and will be trimmed before border is added.

Cutting

From each of five medium/dark print fat quarters, cut:
- Four 8½" squares for alternate blocks

From each of nine medium/dark print fat quarters, cut:
- One 13" square. Cut the squares diagonally into quarters for a total of eighteen side triangles.
- One 8" square. Cut the squares in half diagonally for a total of four corner triangles.

Assembly

1. Referring to the quilt center assembly diagram, sew the star blocks, alternate blocks, and side triangles together in diagonal rows. Press the seam allowances in alternating directions by rows so the seams will fit snugly together with less bulk.

2. Pin the rows at the block intersections and sew the rows together. Press the seam allowances in one direction.

3. Sew the corner triangles to the quilt center; press.

4. Trim away the excess fabric from the side and corner triangles, taking care to allow a ¼" seam allowance beyond the corners of each block.

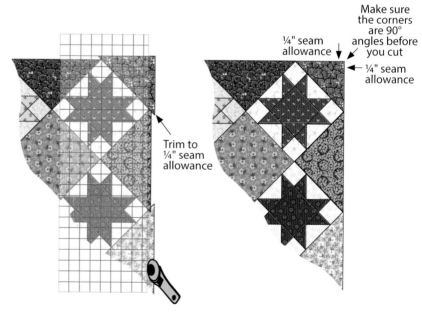

Trimming side and corner triangles

Adding the Borders

Note: The yardage given allows for the border strips to be cut on the crosswise grain.

Cutting
From the large floral print, cut:
- Eight 6½" x 42" border strips. Attach the 6½"-wide large floral border strips.

Piecing
Diagonally piece the strips together as needed.

Putting It All Together

Cut a 5-yard length of backing fabric in half crosswise to make two 2½-yard lengths. Quilt as desired.

Binding

Cutting
From the diagonal print, cut:
- Eight 2¾" x 42" strips.

Sew the binding to the quilt using a ⅜" seam allowance.

Quilt center assembly diagram

Friends and Flowers

Designed by Suzanne McNeill, pieced by Donna Perrotta, quilted by Julie Lawson
Finished size: 49½" x 61¾" (126 x 157cm)

Basic shapes and bold primary colors make this a perfect quilt for a nursery, playroom, or child's bedroom. Simple piecing provides an excellent start for beginners and makes this quilt a choice candidate for the many community service projects which endeavor to supply quilts for hospitals and homeless shelters.

Materials

We used one layer cake. You'll need a total of thirty-two 10" squares:
- Four red or ⅓ yard
- Four blue or ⅓ yard
- Four green or ⅓ yard
- Three yellow or ⅓ yard
- Three striped or ⅓ yard
- Eight white or ⅝ yard
- Two black or ⅓ yard
- Four plaid or ⅓ yard
- ¼ yard black with dots for Border 1
- 1¾ yards red print for Border 2 and binding
- 2⅞ yards backing fabric
- 58" x 70" batting
- Eight yellow 1" buttons (not for children)
- Green pearl cotton or 6-ply floss
- #22 chenille needle
- Fusible web (such as Steam-A-Seam 2®) for appliqués (optional)
- Template plastic and templates on pages 154–155

Cutting and Sorting

Cut and set aside the following deepest colors for sashing strips:
- Two red
- Three blue
- Three green
- Three yellow

Cut and set aside the lightest colors to make block centers:
- Eight white
- Four plaid

Cut and set aside these colors for appliqués:
- One green
- Two red
- Two black
- One blue

Cut and set aside three stripes for corner squares.

Block Centers
Cut eight white and four plaid 10" squares.

Corner Squares
Cut twenty striped 3¼" squares.

Sashings
Cut the following 3¼" x 10" strips: six red, nine blue, eight green, eight yellow.

Quilt Top Assembly

1. Arrange all blocks, corner squares, and sashing strips on a work surface.

2. Position the corner squares so the stripes are horizontal.

3. Refer to the quilt assembly diagram on page 97 for block placement and color.

4. Sew the pieces for each row together. Press.

5. Sew the rows together. Press.

Quilt originally appeared in *Big Blocks, Big Quilts*

Adding the Borders

Border 1

1. Cut five strips 1½" x 42" on the crosswise grain.

2. Sew the strips together end to end.

3. Cut two strips 1½" x 52¼" for the sides.

4. Cut two strips 1½" x 42" for the top and bottom.

5. Sew the side borders to the quilt. Press.

6. Sew the top and bottom borders to the quilt. Press.

Border 2

1. Cut the strips parallel to the selvage to eliminate piecing.

2. Cut two strips 4½" x 54¼" for the sides.

3. Cut two strips 4½" x 50" for the top and bottom.

4. Sew the side borders to the quilt. Press.

5. Sew top and bottom borders to the quilt. Press.

Making the Appliqués

Use the desired method of appliqué.
Stems: Make running stitches with green pearl cotton or 6-ply floss and a chenille needle.

Basic Turned-Edge Method

1. Trace the templates on pages 154–155 onto template plastic and cut out.

2. Trace and cut out each fabric shape, leaving a scant ¼" fabric border all around, and clip the curves.

3. Place the template plastic on the wrong side of the fabric. Spray edges with starch.

4. Press the ¼" border over the edge of the template plastic with the tip of a hot iron. Press firmly.

5. Remove the template, maintaining the folded edge on the back of the fabric.

6. Position the shape on the quilt and blind-stitch in place.

Basic Needle-Turn Method

1. Trace the templates on pages 154–155 onto template plastic and cut out.

2. Trace and cut out each fabric shape, leaving a ¼" fabric border all around.

3. Baste the shapes to the quilt, keeping the basting stitches away from the edge of the fabric. Begin with all areas that are under other layers and work to the topmost layer.

4. For an area no more than 2" ahead of where you are working, trim to ⅛" and clip the curves.

5. Using the needle, roll the edge under and sew tiny blind stitches to secure.

Using Fusible Web for Iron-On Appliqué

1. Trace the template onto Steam-A-Seam 2® fusible web.

2. Press the templates onto the wrong side of the fabric.

3. Cut out templates exactly on the drawn line.

4. Score the web paper with a pin, then remove the paper.

5. Position the fabric, fusible side down, on the quilt. Press with a hot iron following the manufacturer's instructions for the fusible web.

6. Stitch around the edge by hand.

Optional: Stabilize the wrong side of the fabric with your favorite stabilizer.
　　Use a size 80 machine-embroidery needle. Fill the bobbin with lightweight basting thread. Thread the machine with a machine-embroidery thread that complements the color being appliquéd.
　　Set your machine for a zigzag stitch and adjust the thread tension if needed. Use a scrap to experiment with different stitch widths and lengths until you find the one you like best.
　　Sew slowly.

Finishing

Quilting
Quilt as desired.

Binding
Cut strips 2½" wide.
Sew them together end to end to equal 243" and refer to the binding instructions starting on page 58 or page 64.

Buttons
After quilting and binding, sew a button to each flower center.

Note: Do not use buttons on quilts intended for babies and young children. Embroider a center with floss instead.

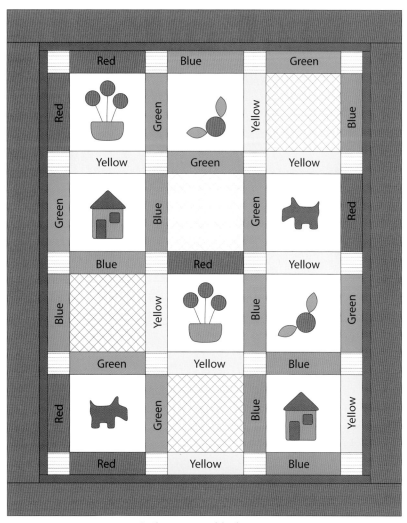

Quilt top assembly diagram

Solid Squares

By Mary M. Hogan
Finished size: Approximately
55" x 66" (140 x 168cm)

A growing collection of solid
fabrics inspired the Solid
Squares quilt. Alternating
white and solid 1½" strings
creates an interesting
design. Square and half-
square triangle blocks were
used to construct the quilt.
The square string blocks
are set on point while the
half-square string blocks
are used for setting and
corner triangles.

Materials

- Seventy-one 8½" square foundations
- 3¼ yards solid white fabric for blocks
- 4¼ yards assorted light to medium solid
  fabrics for blocks

Note: The featured quilt uses fifteen to twenty
different solids

- ½ yard binding fabric
- 3½ yards backing fabric
- Batting

Note: Fabric requirements may vary depending
on the width and placement of strings.

WOF = width of fabric
Fabric is 42"–44" wide unless otherwise noted.

Cutting

From all of the solid
fabrics, cut:
- 1½" x WOF strings

From the backing fabric, cut:
- One 74" x WOF piece
- Two 24" x WOF pieces

From the binding fabric, cut:
- Seven 2½" x WOF strips

Note: The featured quilt
uses four solid fabrics for
the binding.

Design Elements	
Unifying elements	• Same strip width used throughout • Repeating white solids
Variation	• Varying solid fabrics
Color	• Assorted colors • Light to medium value
Line and shape	• Blocks set on point resemble squares within squares

Quilt originally appeared in *String Quilt Style*

Making the Blocks

Note: Sew with a careful ¼" seam allowance. To create the quilt design, the solid and white strings need to line up when the blocks are sewn together.

Making Diagonal String Blocks

1. Draw a diagonal line ¼" from the center of a foundation square.

2. Place a solid-colored string right side up on the foundation square, matching the right raw edge of the string with the drawn line. Make sure the string extends past the corners of the foundation square. Secure with pins if desired.

3. Lay another solid-colored string right side down on the first string, matching the right edges.

4. Sew the strings together along the right edge using a ¼" seam allowance. Press the string open. The two strings are now centered in the block.

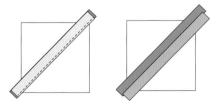

5. Sew a solid white string to either side of the sewn strings. Press the strings open.

6. Continue adding solid-colored and white strings to each side of the foundation, alternating the string colors. Press strings open.

7. Each foundation square should end with solid white strings in the corners. Make a total of forty-nine diagonal string blocks.

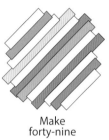

Make
forty-nine

Making Single Half-Square Triangle Blocks

Note: You will be sewing strings to only one side of the foundation square.

1. Draw a diagonal line ¼" from the center of a foundation square, as shown.

2. Place a solid-colored string right side up on the foundation square, matching the left raw edge of the string with the drawn line. Make sure the string extends past the corners of the foundation square. Secure with pins if desired.

3. Lay a solid white string right side down on the first string, matching the right edges.

4. Sew the strings together along the right edge using a ¼" seam allowance. Press the string open.

5. Sew a solid-colored string to the right side of the sewn strings. Press the string open.

6. Continue adding solid and white strings to the right side of the foundation, alternating the string colors. Press strings open.

7. Each foundation square should end with a solid white string in the corner. Make a total of twenty-two half-square triangle blocks.

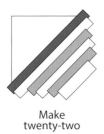

Make
twenty-two

Quilt Top Assembly

1. Press blocks carefully, using starch if needed to stabilize the blocks.

2. Trim diagonal string blocks to 8½" square.

3. Trim the half-square triangle blocks along the edges of the foundation square. Do not trim any fabric extending on the left side of the foundation.

4. Remove the foundation papers.

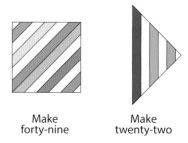

Make
forty-nine

Make
twenty-two

5. Referring to the quilt top assembly diagram, lay out the diagonal string blocks and half-square triangle blocks in diagonal rows.

Note: Two pairs of half-square triangles will be added to the corners after the diagonal rows are joined together.

6. Using ¼" seams, sew the blocks together in diagonal rows, aligning each block's solid white and colored strings with the block next to it. Press seams open.

7. Sew the diagonal rows together.

8. Sew pairs of half-square triangles to the remaining corners to complete the quilt top.

Finishing

1. Sew the two 24" x WOF pieces together end to end to make a 24" x 84" piece.

2. Sew the 74" x WOF backing piece to the 24" x 84" piece as shown. Press seams open.

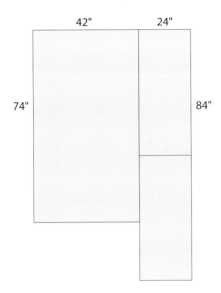

3. Trim away any excess length.

4. Layer the backing, batting and quilt top together and baste. Quilt as desired.

5. Sew the binding strips together using diagonal seams to create one continuous strip. Press the strip in half lengthwise, wrong sides together, and sew to the raw edge of the quilt top. Fold binding over raw edges and hand-stitch in place.

Quilt top assembly diagram

Wee Play Rainbow

Designed by Suzanne McNeill, pieced by Donna Perrotta, quilted by Julie Lawson
Finished size: 57" x 66" (145 x 168cm)

Playful and lighthearted, this quilt takes us back to the fun-filled days of our youth. Capture a rainbow of color in a delightful project that will draw out the child in everyone, young and old. This is a good choice for a group project because you can easily distribute the squares, allowing each person to make just a few blocks.

Materials

We used one layer cake. You'll need a total of thirty-two 10" squares:
- Seven red or ⅝ yard
- Two light orange or ⅓ yard
- Two dark orange or ⅓ yard
- Five yellow or ⅝ yard
- Six green or ⅝ yard
- Six light blue or ⅝ yard
- Four blue or ⅓ yard

¼ yard dark blue for Border 1
1¾ yards multi-stripe for Border 2 and binding
3½ yards backing fabric
65" x 74" batting

Cutting and Sorting

Set aside the following 10" squares to make half-square triangles:
- Seven red
- Four orange
- Five yellow
- Five green
- Seven light blue
- Five dark blue

Making the Blocks

Half-Square Triangle Blocks

1. Pair up two 10" square colors (refer to the diagram on page 105).

2. Draw a line from corner to corner on the diagonal.

3. Sew a seam ¼" on each side of the diagonal line.

4. Cut apart on the diagonal line to make two squares; press.

5. Center and trim all blocks to 9½" x 9½".

6. Make thirty half-square triangles.

Half-square triangles
Each pair makes two squares

Quilt originally appeared in *Big Blocks, Big Quilts*

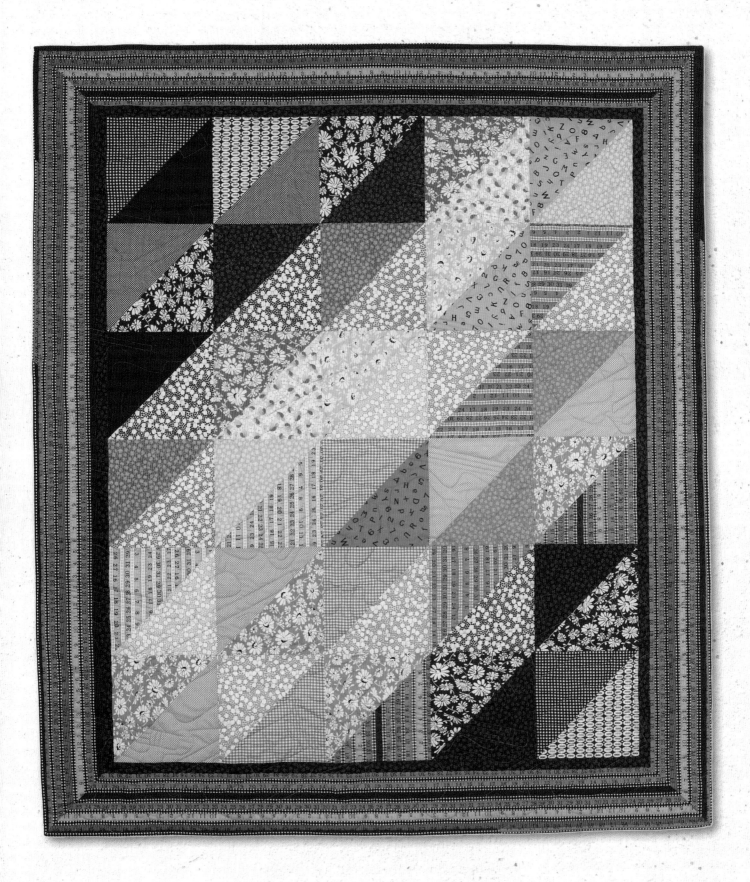

Triangle Blocks

Set aside the following 10" squares to make triangle blocks, and cut each square listed on the diagonal.
- Three red
- Three yellow
- One blue
- One light blue

Mix up the pieces so you get the following:
- Three yellow-yellow with different prints
- Three red-red with different prints
- One light blue-blue

Tip: Handle the pieces carefully to avoid stretching along the diagonal.

1. Pair up two triangles.

2. Sew a seam ¼" from the diagonal.

3. Open the block and press.

4. Center and trim to 9½" x 9½".

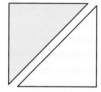

Triangle blocks: cut and then sew.

Quilt Top Assembly

1. Arrange all blocks on a work surface or table. Refer to the diagram for block placement and direction.

2. Sew the blocks together in six rows, five blocks per row. Press.

3. Sew the rows together. Press.

Adding the Borders

Border 1

1. Cut five strips 1½" x 42" on the crosswise grain.

2. Sew the strips together end to end.

3. Cut two strips 1½" x 54½" for the sides.

4. Cut two strips 1½" x 47½" for the top and bottom.

5. Sew the side borders to the quilt. Press.

6. Sew the top and bottom borders to the quilt. Press.

Mitered Border 2:

1. Cut the strips parallel to the selvage to eliminate piecing on the long borders.

2. Cut two strips 5½" x 66½" for the sides.

3. Cut two strips 5½" x 57½" for the top and bottom.

4. Center a side border strip along each side of the quilt, allowing 5½" to hang off each edge for mitering.

5. Repeat for the top and bottom border strips.

6. See the instructions for mitered borders on the facing page.

Finishing

Quilting
Quilt as desired.

Binding
Cut strips 2½" wide.
Sew the strips together end to end to equal 256".
Refer to the binding instructions starting on page 58 or page 64.

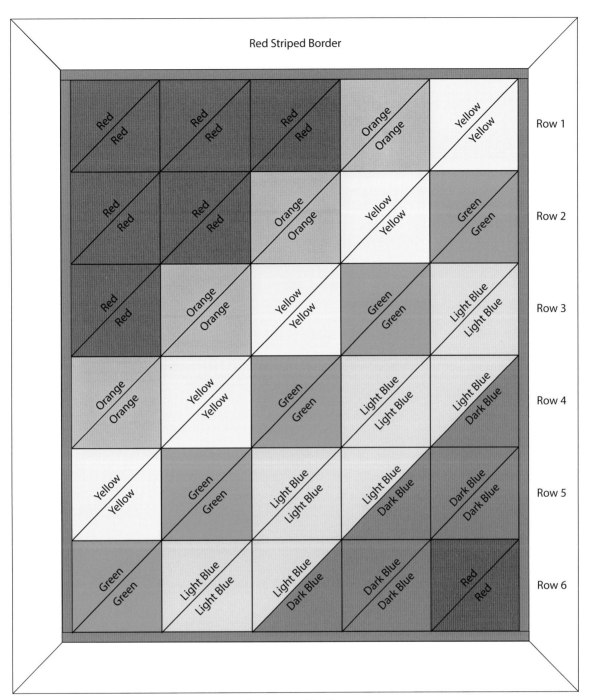

Red Striped Border

Row 1
Row 2
Row 3
Row 4
Row 5
Row 6

Quilt top assembly diagram

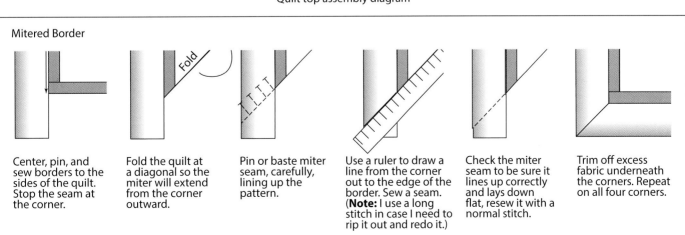

Mitered Border

Center, pin, and sew borders to the sides of the quilt. Stop the seam at the corner.

Fold the quilt at a diagonal so the miter will extend from the corner outward.

Pin or baste miter seam, carefully, lining up the pattern.

Use a ruler to draw a line from the corner out to the edge of the border. Sew a seam. (**Note:** I use a long stitch in case I need to rip it out and redo it.)

Check the miter seam to be sure it lines up correctly and lays down flat, resew it with a normal stitch.

Trim off excess fabric underneath the corners. Repeat on all four corners.

Party for Punch

Designed by Suzanne McNeill, pieced by
Kayleen Allen, quilted by Sue Needle
Finished size: 48" x 67" (122 x 170cm)

It's like opening a new box of
crayons or going on a spending
spree at the fabric shop! Prepare
to brighten your spaces. You're
going to love the ease with
which these blocks go together.
Primary colors pack a punch
that complements your decor
all year round. Enjoy this one in
the family room or out on the
porch swing.

	Choose a Quilt Size				
			YARDAGE		
	Color	Location	Throw 48" x 67"	Double 67" x 86"	King 113" x 113"
Fabric A	Assorted prints	Corners	1¾ yards	3⅜ yards	7 yards
Fabric B	Very dark print	Block centers	⅝ yard	1½ yards	3⅛ yards
Fabric C	Dark print	Border 1	¼ yard	⅓ yard	¾ yard
Fabric D	Medium print	Border 2 and binding	1¾ yards	2¼ yards	3¼ yards
	Cut Size	**Location**			
Block A	10" square	Corners	24 assorted prints	48 assorted prints	100 prints
Block B	10" square	Block centers	6 dark prints	12 dark prints	25 dark prints
		Border 1	Two 1½" x 57½	Two 1½" x 76½"	Two 2½" x 95½"
			Two 1½" x 40½"	Two 1½" x 59½"	Two 2½" x 99½"
		Border 2 and binding	Two 4½" x 59½	Two 4½" x 78½"	Two 7½" x 99½"
			Two 4½" x 48½"	Two 4½" x 67½"	Two 7½" x 113½"

Quilt originally appeared in *10-Minute Blocks*

Cutting

We used a layer cake collection of pre-cut 10" squares to get an assortment of thirty assorted prints (eight blue, eight green, four yellow, four orange, and six very dark red).

Refer to the chart on page 106 for yardage and cutting. WOF = width of fabric

Making the Blocks

Refer to Basic Instructions for Ten-Minute Blocks on pages 18–19. Make six. We made two blue, two green, one yellow, and one orange with red centers.

Quilt Center Assembly

1. Arrange and sew two large blocks per row.

2. Sew the sets of blocks together in three rows. Press.

Borders

Border 1

1. Cut five strips 1½" x WOF.

2. Cut two strips 1½" x 57½" for the sides.

3. Cut two strips 1½" x 40½" for the top and bottom.

4. Sew the side borders to the quilt. Press.

5. Sew the top and bottom borders to the quilt. Press.

Border 2

1. Cut 4½" strips parallel to the selvage to prevent piecing.

2. Cut two strips 4½" x 59½" for the sides.

3. Cut two strips 4½" x 48½" for the top and bottom.

4. Sew thee side borders to the quilt. Press.

5. Sew the top and bottom borders to the quilt. Press.

Finishing

Quilting

Quilt as desired.

Binding

1. Cut strips 2½" wide.

2. Sew the strips together end to end to equal 240".

3. Refer to the binding instructions starting on page 58 or page 64.

These instructions are for a throw quilt, 48" x 67". (Refer to the chart on page 106 for other sizes.)

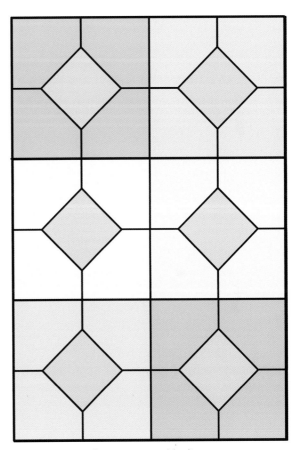

Quilt center assembly diagram

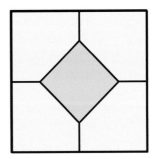

Large block: make six
Use four squares of similar color/tone with an accent color in the center.

Baby Girl and Baby Boy

By Lynette Jensen
Finished size: 56" x 56" (142 x 142cm)

A book of baby quilts would not be complete without a project in the traditional baby pastels of blush pink and powder blue, and this design throws brown into the mix for a bit of contrast. Baby Girl and Baby Boy arc constructed in the same way; just pick the color that complements your little one's nursery and get stitching.

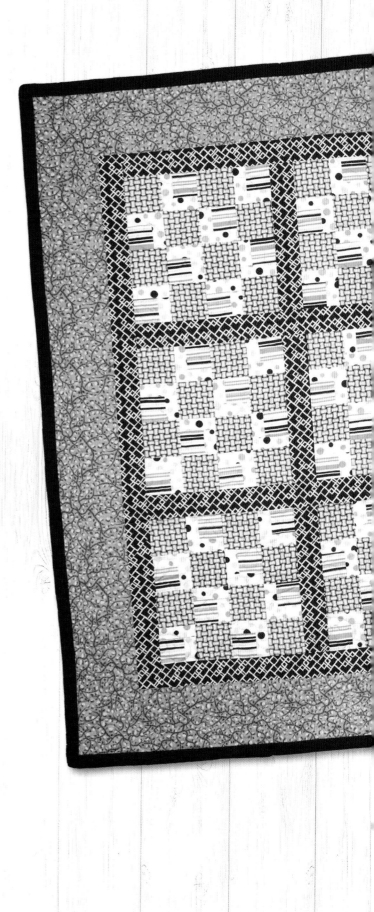

Materials

Pink quilt
- ½ yard pink/brown stripe for blocks
- ⅝ yard pink/brown dot for blocks
- ⅞ yard pink/brown weave print for blocks
- ¾ yard brown/pink geometric print for lattice, inner border
- 1¼ yards pink print for outer border
- 1⅓ yards brown solid for wide binding
- 3½ yards for backing
- Quilt batting, at least 62" square

Blue quilt
- ½ yard blue/brown stripe for blocks
- ⅝ yard blue/brown dot for blocks
- ⅞ yard blue/brown weave print for blocks
- ¾ yard brown/blue geometric print for lattice, inner border
- 1¼ yards blue print for outer border
- 1⅓ yards brown solid for wide binding
- 3½ yards for backing
- Quilt batting, at least 62" square

Quilt originally appeared in *Thimbleberries® Small Wonders*

Making the Blocks

Makes nine blocks

Cutting

From the pink/brown (or blue/brown) stripe, cut:
- Five 2½" x 44" strips

From the pink/brown (or blue/brown) dot, cut:
- Three 3½" x 44" strips. From the strips, subcut: seventy-two 1½" x 3½" rectangles
- Five 1½" x 44" strips

From the pink/brown (or blue/brown) weave print, cut:
- Seven 3½" x 44" strips. From the strips, subcut: seventy-two 3½" squares

Piecing

Refer to the arrows on the diagrams for pressing.

1. Aligning the long edges, sew together the 1½" x 44" pink/brown (or blue/brown) dot strips and the 2½" x 44" pink/brown (or blue/brown) stripe strips in pairs; press. Make five strip sets. Cut the strip sets into segments. Sew a 1½" x 3½" pink/brown (or blue/brown) dot rectangle to the right edge of each unit; press. At this point, each unit should measure 3½" square.

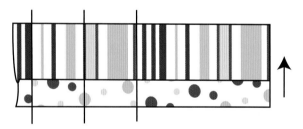

Crosscut seventy-two 2½-wide segments

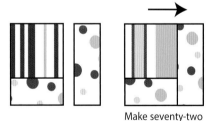

Make seventy-two

2. Referring to the block diagram, sew together eight Step 1 units and eight 3½" pink/brown (or blue/brown) weave print squares in four rows; press. Sew the rows together; press. At this point, each block should measure 12½" square.

Note: Pay close attention to the Step 1 block placement.

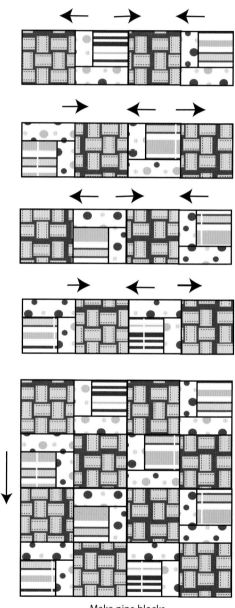

Make nine blocks

Making the Quilt Center

Cutting

From the brown/pink (or brown/blue) geometric print, cut:

- Four 2½" x 44" strips. From the strips, subcut: two 2½" x 40½" lattice strips
- Six 2½" x 12½" lattice segments

Quilt Center Assembly

1. Referring to quilt assembly diagram on page 112 or 113, sew together three of the pieced blocks and two of the 2½" x 12½" brown/pink (or brown/blue) geometric print lattice segments; press. Make three block rows. At this point, each block row should measure 12½" x 40½".

2. Sew together the block rows and the 2½" x 40½" brown/pink (or brown/blue) geometric print lattice strips; press. At this point, the quilt center should measure 40½" square.

Borders

Note: Yardage given allows for border strips to be cut on crosswise grain. Diagonally piece the strips as needed.

Cutting

From the brown/pink (or brown/blue) geometric print, cut:

- Five 2½" x 44" inner border strips

From the pink (or blue) print, cut:

- Six 6½" x 44" outer border strips

Attaching the Borders

1. Attach the 2½"-wide brown/pink (or brown/blue) geometric print inner border strips.

2. Attach the 6½"-wide pink (or blue) outer border strips.

Putting It All Together

Cut the 3½-yard length of backing fabric in half crosswise to make two 1¾-yard lengths. Quilt as desired.

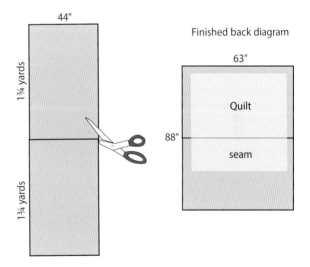

Finished back diagram

Binding

1. From the brown solid, cut seven 6½" x 44" strips.

2. Sew the binding to the quilt using a scant 1" seam allowance. This measurement will produce a 1"-wide finished double binding.

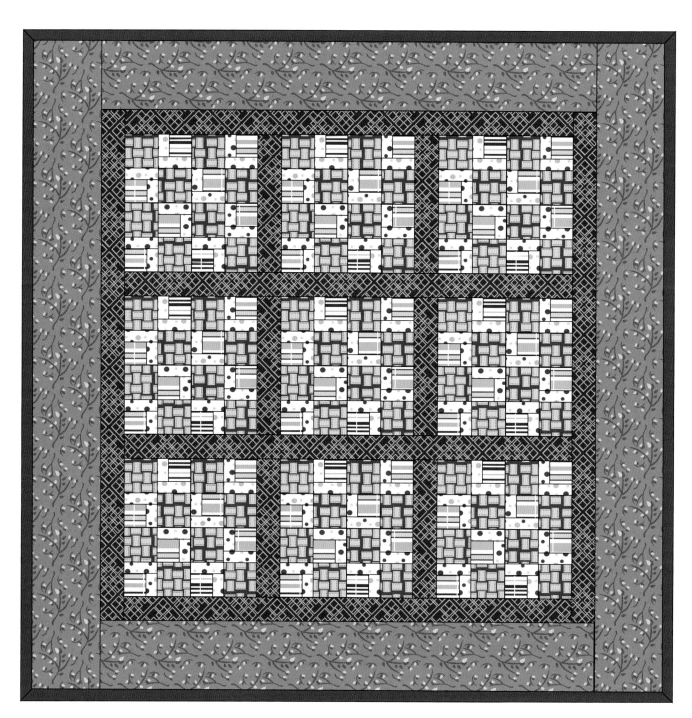

Baby Girl quilt top assembly diagram

Baby Boy quilt top assembly diagram

Hey Little Sister

Designed by McB McManus and
E.B. Updegraff, pieced and quilted
by Sue Voegtlin

Finished size: Approximately 52¾" x 60½"
(134 x 154cm)

Gray and pink . . . what a pretty
pair! Add a geometric heart made
from squares and half-square
triangles in pink shades from deep
to pastel, and you have a sweet
welcome for the family's newest
bundle of joy.

Materials

- 1¾ yards pink print fabric
- 1⅝ yards gray dot fabric
- One fat eighth each of light,
  medium, and dark solid
  pink fabric
- 3½ yards backing fabric
- ½ yard binding fabric
- 57" x 65" batting

WOF = width of fabric
LOF = length of fabric
Fabric quantities based on 42"–
44"-wide, 100% cotton fabrics
Fat eighth = 9" x 22"

Cutting

From the pink print fabric, cut:
- One 4½" x LOF strip
- One 24½" x LOF strip

From the gray dot fabric, cut:
- One 24½" x 36½" strip
- Two 4½" x WOF strips. From each
  strip, subcut:
  - One 4½" x 24½" strip
  - One 4½" x 16½" strip

- Two 4½" squares
- Four 5" squares

From each solid pink fat eighth, cut:
- Two 4½" squares
- Two 5" squares

From the binding fabric, cut:
- Six 2½" x WOF strips

Quilt originally appeared in *Easy-Cut Baby Quilts*

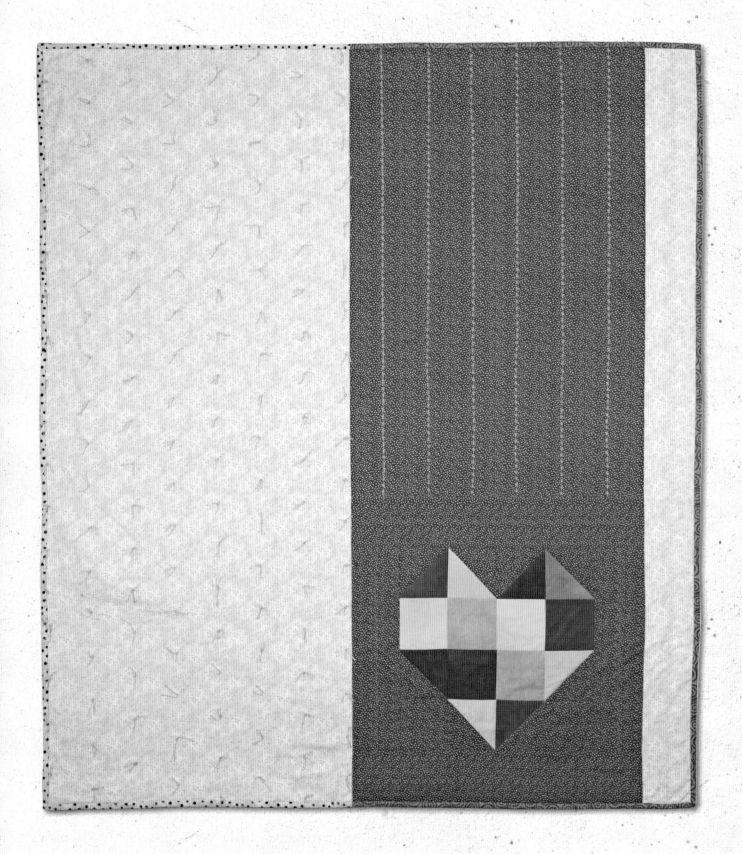

Making the Heart Block

1. Lay a 5" dark pink square on a gray dot square, right sides together.

2. Draw a diagonal line from corner to corner on the wrong side of the top square. Sew a ¼" on either side of the drawn line.

3. Cut on the drawn line. Press the seams open to make two dark pink/gray dot half-square triangles. Make a total of four dark pink/gray dot half-square triangles.

Make four

4. Referring to Steps 1–3, make a total of four light pink/gray dot half-square triangles and two medium pink/gray dot half-square triangles.

Note: You will only use three light pink/gray dot half-square triangles and one medium pink/gray dot half-square triangle.

Make
four

Make
two

5. Lay out the half-square triangles and 4½" squares in rows as shown.

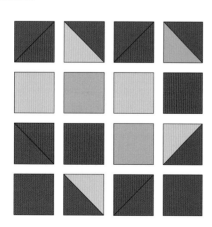

6. Sew the pieces together in rows.

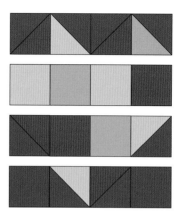

7. Sew the rows together to complete the heart block.

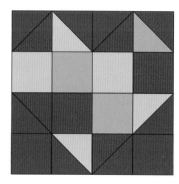

Quilt Top Assembly

1. Sew the gray dot 4½" x 16½" strips to opposite sides of the heart block. Press.

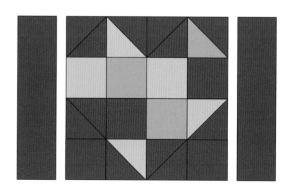

2. Sew the gray dot 4½" x 24½" strips to the remaining sides of the heart block. Press.

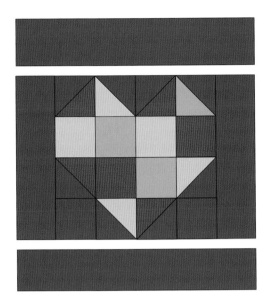

3. Sew the 24½" x 36½" gray dot strip to the top of the heart block to complete the heart panel. Press.

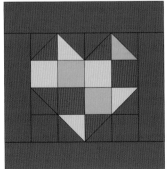

4. Referring to the quilt assembly diagram, sew the pink print 4½" x LOF strip to the right side of the heart panel. Press.

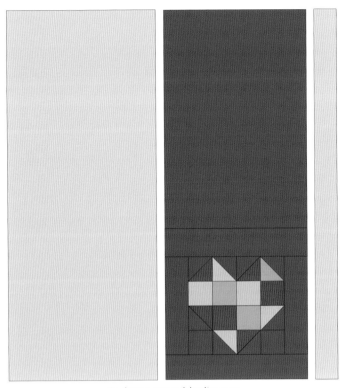

Quilt top assembly diagram

5. Sew the pink print 24½" x LOF strip to the left side of the heart panel. Press.

6. Trim any excess fabric even with the heart panel.

Finishing

1. Layer the backing, batting, and quilt top. Baste the layers together and quilt as desired.

2. Sew the 2½"-wide binding strips together to make one continuous strip. Press the strip in half lengthwise, wrong sides together. Sew the binding to the front of the quilt, aligning the raw edges. Turn the binding over the edge to the back of the quilt and hand- or machine-stitch in place.

Daisy Chain

By Lynette Jensen
Finished size: 63" x 63" (160 x 160cm)

A combination of nine-patch blocks, pieced blocks with half-square triangles, and solid squares in pretty pastels results in a crisp geometric design with a classic look.

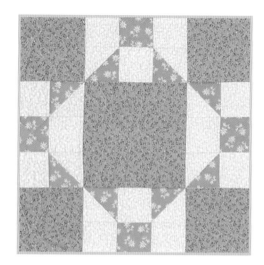

Materials

- 1 yard green print for blocks
- ¾ yard yellow print for block centers, inner border
- 1¼ yards beige print for background
- 2 yards rose print for alternate blocks, outer border
- ⅔ yard yellow print for binding
- 4 yards for backing
- Quilt batting, at least 69" square

Making Nine-Patch Blocks

Makes eight blocks

Cutting
From the green print, cut:
- Four 3½" x 44" strips
From the yellow print, cut:
- One 3½" x 44" strip
From the beige print, cut:
- Four 3½" x 44" strips

Piecing
Refer to the arrows on the diagrams for pressing.

1. Aligning the long edges, sew 3½" x 44" green strips to both side edges of the 3½" x 44" yellow strip. Press the strip set, then cut the strip set into segments.

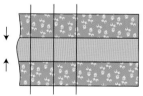

Crosscut eight 3½"-wide segments

2. Aligning the long edges, sew 3½" x 44" beige strips to both side edges of a 3½" x 44" green strip. Make two strip sets; press. Cut the strip sets into segments.

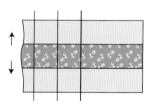

Crosscut sixteen 3½"-wide segments

3. Sew Step 2 segments to top/bottom edges of the Step 1 units; press. At this point, each nine-patch block should measure 9½" square.

Make eight

Quilt originally appeared in *Thimbleberries® Small Wonders*

Making the Pieced Blocks

Makes twelve blocks

Cutting

From the green print, cut:
- Three 3⅞" x 44" strips
- One 3½" x 44" strip

From the beige print, cut:
- Three 3⅞" x 44" strips
- Two 3½" x 44" strips
- Two more 3½" x 44" strips. From the strips, subcut: twenty-four 3½" squares

Piecing

Refer to the arrows on the diagrams for pressing.

1. Aligning the long edges, sew 3½" x 44" beige strips to both side edges of the 3½" x 44" green strip; press. Cut the strip set into segments.

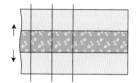

Crosscut twelve 3½"-wide segments

2. With right sides together, layer the 3⅞" x 44" green and beige strips in pairs. Press together, but do not sew. Cut the layered strips into squares. Cut the layered squares in half diagonally to make forty-eight sets of triangles. Stitch ¼" from the diagonal edge of each pair of triangles; press.

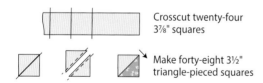

Crosscut twenty-four 3⅞" squares

Make forty-eight 3½" triangle-pieced squares

3. Sew the Step 2 triangle-pieced squares to both side edges of a 3½" beige square; press.

Make twenty-four

4. Sew the Step 3 units to the top/bottom edges of the Step 1 segments; press. At this point, each pieced block should measure 9½" square.

Make twelve

Making the Quilt Center

Cutting

From rose print, cut:
- Two 9½" x 44" strips. From the strips, cut: five 9½" alternate block squares

Quilt Center Assembly

1. Referring to quilt center assembly diagram for placement, lay out the nine-patch blocks, pieced blocks, and alternate blocks in five rows with five blocks in each row.

2. Sew the blocks together in each row. Press the seam allowances in alternating directions by rows so the seams will fit snugly together with less bulk. At this point, each block row should measure 9½" x 45½".

3. Pin the rows together at the block intersections; stitch and press. At this point, the quilt center should measure 45½" square.

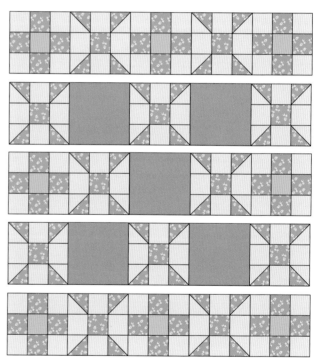

Quilt center assembly diagram

Borders

Note: The yardage given allows for the border strips to be cut on crosswise grain. Diagonally piece strips as needed.

Cutting

From the yellow print, cut:
- Five 3½" x 44" inner border strips

From the rose print, cut:
- Seven 6½" x 44" outer border strips

Attaching the Borders

Press the border strips toward the borders just added.

1. Attach 3½"-wide yellow inner border strips.

2. Attach 6½"-wide rose outer border strips.

Putting It All Together

Cut a 4-yard length of backing fabric in half crosswise to make two 2-yard lengths. Quilt as desired.

Binding

Cutting

From the yellow print, cut:
- Seven 2¾" x 44" strips

Sew the binding to the quilt using a ⅜" seam allowance. This measurement will produce a ½"-wide finished double binding.

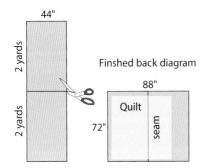

Finshed back diagram

Quilt top assembly diagram

Baby Cakes

Designed by Suzanne McNeill,
pieced and quilted by Donna Kinsey
Finished size: 42" x 52" (107 x 132cm)

Jelly rolls make it possible to complete a quilt top in a weekend. Here are some tips: First, when designing, divide the strips into groups of color. Next, estimate the number of strips you will need for the blocks. If you need an extra strip or two of a color (let's say green), look for a print with a lot of green and move it to the green stack. The same applies for the other colors.

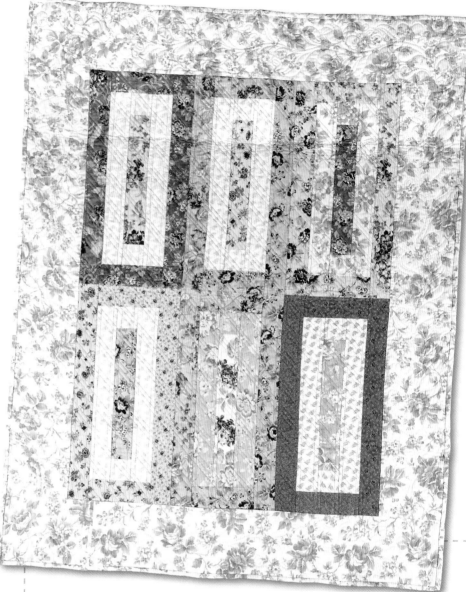

Materials

We used one jelly roll collection of 2½" fabric strips.
- ½ yard purple or four strips 2½" x 42"
- ½ yard ivory or six strips 2½" x 42"
- ½ yard yellow or four strips 2½" x 42"
- ¼ yard green or two strips 2½" x 42"
- ¼ yard pink or three strips 2½" x 42"
- 1½ yards ivory/green print for borders and binding
- 2 yards backing fabric, piece it to 46" x 56"
- 46" x 56" batting

Tips

As a guide for yardage:
- Each ¼ yard, or fat quarter, equals three strips
- A pre-cut jelly roll strip is 2½" x 42"
- Cut fat quarter strips to 2½" x 21"

Quilt originally appeared in *Strip Happy Quilt*

Cutting

Purple: One Strip A for Block 3: 2½" x 12½"
- Four Strips E for Blocks 1 and 6: 2½" x 20½"
- Four Strips D for Blocks 1 and 6: 2½" x 6½"

White: One strip A for Block 5: 2½" x 12½"
- Ten Strips C for Blocks 1, 2, 3, 4, and 6: 2½" x 16½"
- Ten Squares B for Blocks 1, 2, 3, 4, and 6: 2½" x 2½"

Yellow: Two Strips A for Blocks 1 and 2: 2½" x 12½"
- Four Strips E for Blocks 3 and 4: 2½" x 20½"
- Four Strips D for Blocks 3 and 4: 2½" x 6½"

Green: Two Strips A for Blocks 4 and 6: 2½" x 12½"
- Two Strips D for Block 5: 2½" x 6½"
- Two Strips E for Block 5: 2½" x 20½"

Pink: Two Squares B for Block 5: 2½" x 2½"
- Two Strips C for Block 5: 2½" x 16½"
- Two Strips D for Block 2: 2½" x 6½"
- Two Strips E for Block 2: 2½" x 20½"

Block and Quilt Top Assembly

1. See block diagram.

2. Sew one Square B onto each end of Strip A. Press.

3. Sew one Strip C to each side. Press.

4. Sew one Strip D to each end. Press.

5. Sew one Strip E to each side. Press.

6. Sew blocks together to make two rows of three. Press.

7. Sew the rows together. Press.

Borders

1. Cut two side strips 6½" x 40½".

2. Cut two strips 6½" x 42½" for the top and bottom.

3. Sew the sides to the quilt. Press.

4. Add the top and bottom borders. Press.

Finishing

1. Quilt as desired.

2. Cut five strips 2½" x 40" and sew end to end for 192" of binding.

3. Refer to the binding instructions starting on page 58 or page 64.

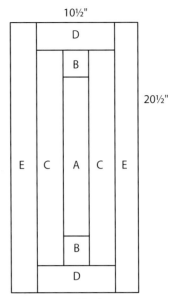

Block assembly diagram

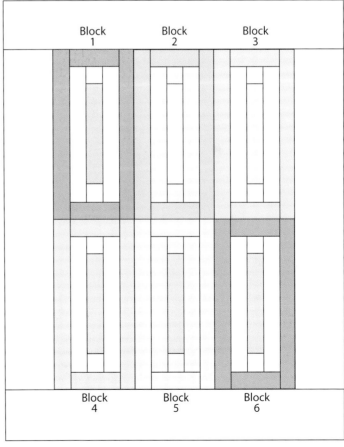

Quilt top assembly diagram

Boogie Woogie

Designed and pieced by Jean Ann Wright, quilted by Sue Bentley (longarm quilting design: Chinook by Denise Schillinger)
Finished size: 54" x 62" (137 x 158cm)

Boogie woogie became popular during the late 1920s. It started as a solo piano style but eventually included guitar, big band, country, and gospel. The blocks in the Boogie Woogie quilt resemble piano keys, and the rows of this quilt are arranged to move up and down as they dance along in musical rows.

Materials

- One jelly roll bundle of forty 2½" x WOF strips
- ½ yard lime green fabric
- ½ yard orange fabric
- ½ yard white fabric
- ¼ yard teal fabric
- 3½ yards backing fabric
- Twin-size batting

Jelly roll bundle = 2½" x WOF strips
WOF = Width of fabric
Note: Sew with a scant ¼" seam allowance

Cutting

Separate the pre-cut strips into ten color groups, with three strips in each group. Set aside seven of the remaining strips for binding.
From the lime green fabric, cut:
- Six 2½" x WOF strips. From the strips, subcut:
  - Thirty-six 2½" x 6½" spacers
From the orange fabric, cut:
- Five 2½" x WOF strips. From the strips, subcut:
  - Twenty-seven 2½" x 6½" spacers

From the white fabric, cut:
- Five 2½" x WOF strips. From the strips, subcut:
  - Twenty-seven 2½" x 6½" spacers
Set nine aside for end spacers.
From the teal fabric, cut:
- Two 2½" x WOF strips. From the strips, subcut:
  - Nine 2½" x 6½" spacers

Quilt originally appeared in *Jelly Roll Jazz*

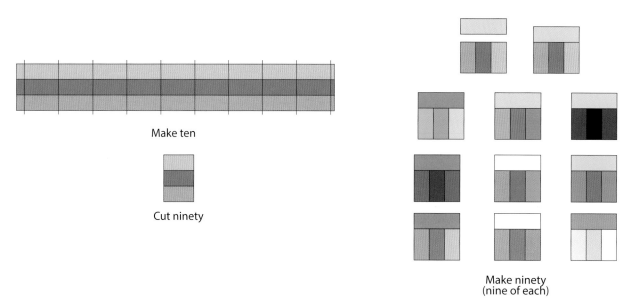

Make ten

Cut ninety

Make ninety
(nine of each)

Row 1   Row 2   Row 3   Row 4   Row 5   Row 6   Row 7   Row 8   Row 9

Quilt top assembly diagram

Flannel Quick Quilt

By Lynette Jensen
Finished size: 56" x 64" (142 x 163cm)

If you're looking for a bright, colorful, and fun quilt project for a little one, look no further! And, as the name says, it's made of cozy flannel, and you can construct it quickly. The design combines a cheerful quilt center surrounded by five borders in complementary prints, and the matching binding pulls it all together.

Materials

- 1⅓ yards orange/green dot flannel for the center panel and Border 4
- ⅓ yard green/brown geometric print for Border 1
- ⅜ yard orange/brown striped flannel for Border 2
- ½ yard green flannel print for the checkerboard border (Border 3)
- 1½ yards yellow/orange geometric print flannel for Border 5
- ½ yard orange/white geometric print flannel for Border 3
- 1⅓ yards orange/brown striped flannel for the wide binding
- 3½ yards for backing
- 62" x 70" or larger batting

Making the Center Panel and Borders

Note: Yardage given allows for border strips to be cut on the crosswise grain. Diagonally piece the strips as needed.

Cutting
From the orange/green dot, cut:
- One 20½" x 28½" center rectangle
- Five 4½" x 44" border strips

From the green/brown geometric print, cut:
- Three 2½" x 44" border strips

From the orange/brown stripe, cut:
- Four 2½" x 44" border strips

From the green print, cut:
- Three 4½" x 44" border strips

From the orange/white geometric print, cut:
- Three 4½" x 44" border strips

From the yellow/orange geometric print, cut:
- Seven 6½" x 44" border strips

Quilt originally appeared in *Thimbleberries® Small Wonders*

Assembling and Attaching the Borders

Press border strips toward borders just added. Refer to the border numbers on the diagram on page 131 for placement.

1. Attach the 2½"-wide green/brown geometric print Border 1 strips to the 20½" x 28½" orange/green dot center panel.

2. Attach the 2½"-wide orange/brown stripe Border 2 strips.

3. Aligning the long edges, sew together the 4½" x 44" green and orange/white geometric print strips in pairs. Make three strip sets. Press the strip sets, then cut them into segments.

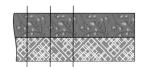

Crosscut twenty 4½"-wide segments

4. For the top/bottom checkerboard borders (Border 3), sew together four of the segments. Remove one of the 4½" green squares from the end of the strip; press. Make two border strips. Sew the checkerboard borders to the top/bottom edges of the quilt center; press.

Make two for top/bottom borders

5. For the side checkerboard borders (Border 3), sew together six of the segments. Remove one of the 4½" orange/white geometric print squares from the end of the strip; press. Make two border strips. Sew the checkerboard borders to the side edges of the quilt center; press.

Make two for side borders

6. Attach the 4½"-wide orange/green dot Border 4 strips.

7. Attach the 6½"-wide yellow/orange geometric print Border 5 strips.

Putting It All Together

Cut a 3½-yard length of backing fabric in half crosswise to make two 1¾-yard lengths. Quilt as desired.

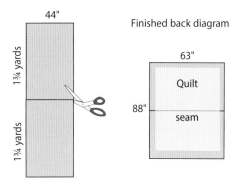

Binding

Cutting

From the orange/brown striped flannel, cut:
- Seven 6½" x 44" strips

Sew the binding to the quilt using a scant 1" seam allowance. This measurement will produce a 1"-wide finished double binding.

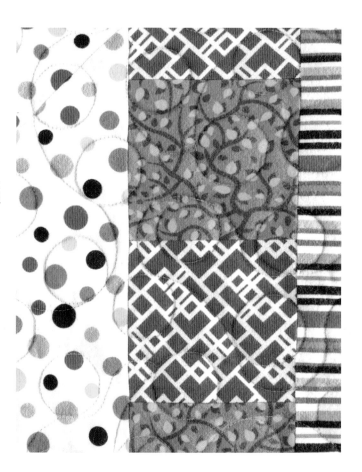

Quilt top assembly diagram

Echoes

Designed and pieced by Jean Ann Wright,
quilted by Robin Kinley
Finished size: 48" x 64" (122 x 163cm)

The star and circle units created with Curvy Log
Cabin blocks are lined up in orderly vertical rows
in the Echoes quilt. The bright fabric hues are
sewn in a somewhat random manner to create a
touch of whimsy.

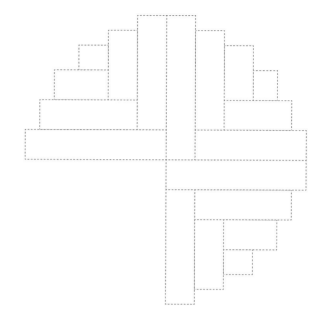

Materials

- One pre-cut bundle of forty
  bright 2½" x WOF strips for
  blocks or 2⅞ yards total assorted
  bright fabrics cut into forty 2½"
  x WOF strips
- One fat quarter each green,
  pink, lime, yellow, and
  light orange
  fabrics for blocks
- 2 yards white fabric for blocks
- ½ yard green binding fabric
- 4¼ yards backing fabric
- Creative Grids® Curvy Log
  Cabin Trim Tool (optional)

WOF = width of fabric
WOFQ = width of fat quarter

Cutting

Note: Refer to the cutting diagrams for 8" blocks on
page 137 to cut the fabric logs to size.
From the white fabric, cut:
- Sixteen 1¾" center squares for
  Block A.
- Cut the remaining fabric into
  1½" x WOF strips for
  Blocks A and B.

From the pink fat quarter, cut:
- Three 1¾" x WOFQ strips.
  From the strips, cut thirty-two 1¾" center squares for
  Block B.

From the assorted fat quarters and the
remaining pink fat quarter, cut:
- 2¼" x WOFQ strips for
  Blocks A and B.

From the green fabric, cut:
- Seven 2¼" x WOF binding strips.

Quilt originally appeared in *Curvy Log Cabin Quilts*

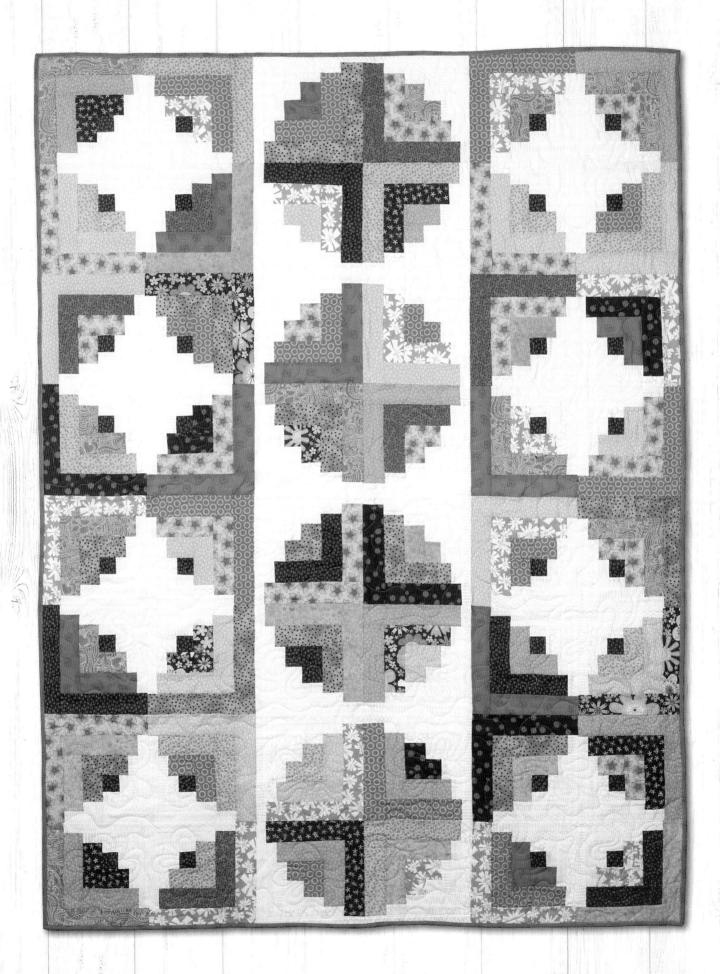

Making the Blocks

Note: Refer to page 136 to sew the blocks together in the right sequence, using the traditional method.

Block A

1. Sew two wide bright strips to adjacent sides of a white center square in a clockwise rotation. Sew two narrow white strips to the remaining sides of the center square, continuing clockwise. This completes Round 1. Press the completed round. Trim Round 1 to size (using the Curvy Log Cabin Trim Tool if desired).

2. Refer to Step 1 to add Rounds 2 and 3 to the block. Press and trim the logs after each round is complete. Make sixteen Blocks A.

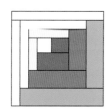

Block A
Make sixteen

Block B

Note: Each round uses matching wide bright print strips.

1. Sew two narrow white strips to adjacent sides of a pink center square in a clockwise rotation. Sew two wide bright strips to the remaining sides of the center square, continuing clockwise. This completes Round 1. Press the completed round. Trim Round 1 to size (using the Curvy Log Cabin Trim Tool if desired).

2. Refer to Step 1 to add Rounds 2 and 3 to the block. Press and trim the logs after each round is complete. Make thirty-two Blocks B.

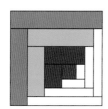

Block B
Make thirty-two

Making the Block Units

1. Lay out four Blocks A as shown. Sew the blocks together in rows. Sew the rows together to make a circle block unit. Make four circle block units.

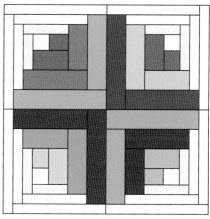

Circle block unit
Make four

2. Lay out four Blocks B as shown. Sew the blocks together in rows. Sew the rows together to make a star block unit. Make eight star block units.

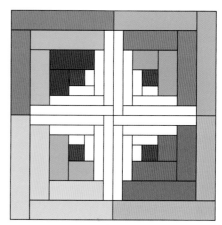

Star block unit
Make eight

Quilt Top Assembly

1. Lay out the block units in three columns as shown. Rows 1 and 3 will each have four star block units, and Row 2 will have four circle block units.

2. Sew the block units together in vertical rows. Sew the rows together to complete the quilt top.

Finishing

1. Layer the quilt top, batting and backing. Quilt as desired.

2. Sew seven 2¼" x WOF green binding strips together end-to-end. Press the strip in half, wrong sides together, along the length. Sew the binding to the edges of the quilt. Turn the binding over the edge to the back and stitch in place.

Quilt top assembly diagram

Making Curvy Log Cabin Blocks the Traditional Way

The Curvy Log Cabin block starts with a precision-cut center square. Wide and narrow fabric logs are then added in a clockwise rotation to make rounds around the square. Each round consists of two wide and two narrow logs. The block is started with the wide logs. Press away from the center square as you add each log.

1. Determine the size of the block you wish to make and use the chart on the facing page to cut the center square and logs to the required size. We are making an 8" finished block in our example, so our center square is 1¾".

   Tip: You may wish to number the logs as you cut them.

2. Sew wide logs 1 and 2 to adjacent sides of the center square in a clockwise rotation.

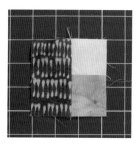

3. Sew narrow logs 3 and 4 to the two remaining adjacent sides of the center square, continuing in a clockwise rotation. This completes Round 1.

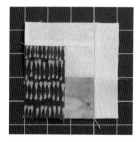

4. Sew wide logs 5 and 6 to adjacent sides of Round 1 in a clockwise rotation.

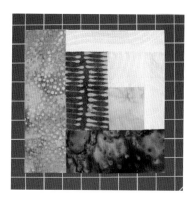

5. Sew narrow logs 7 and 8 to the two remaining adjacent sides of Round 1, continuing in a clockwise rotation. This completes Round 2.

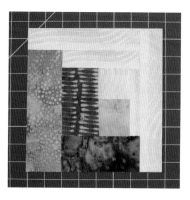

6. Sew two wide (9, 10) and two narrow (11, 12) logs in a clockwise rotation to Round 2 to complete the Curvy Log Cabin block. Press using spray starch or fabric stabilizer.

Cut-to-size diagram for 6" Curvy Log Cabin Block A

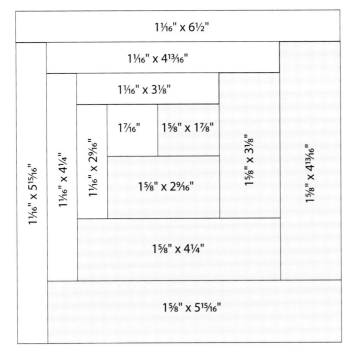

Cut-to-size diagram for 6" Curvy Log Cabin Block B

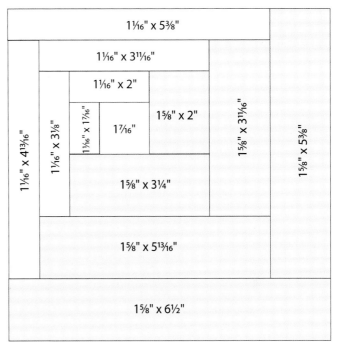

Cut-to-size diagram for 8" Curvy Log Cabin Block A

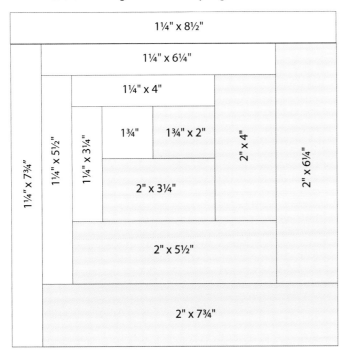

Cut-to-size diagram for 8" Curvy Log Cabin Block B

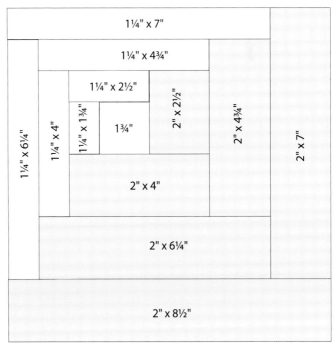

Moon and Stars

By McB McManus and E.B. Updegraff
Finished size: Approximately
42" x 65" (107 x 165cm)

Good night, baby! You can put this dreamy design together fairly quickly, as the quilt body is one large piece of fabric accented by a large moon and star appliqués in multiple sizes.

Materials

- 2 yards gray print fabric
- Four fat quarters in assorted white prints
- One fat quarter in yellow print fabric
- 3½ yards backing fabric
- ½ yard binding fabric
- 1¼ yards fusible web
- 50" x 73" batting
- Template plastic and templates on pages 156–157

WOF = width of fabric
Fabric quantities based on 42"–44"-wide, 100% cotton fabrics
Fat quarter = 18" x 22"

Cutting

Trim the gray print fabric to approximately 65" long.
From the binding fabric, cut: Six 2½" x WOF binding strips

Making and Placing the Appliqués

Note: The appliqué shapes have been reversed for you.

1. Trace the moon and star templates on pages 156–157 onto the paper side of the fusible web. Trace the templates in the numbers given.
- One moon
- Five large stars
- Nine medium stars
- Twenty-three small stars

2. Cut out the shapes, leaving approximately ¼" of web beyond the outside of each shape.

Quilt originally appeared in *Easy-Cut Baby Quilts*

3. Fuse the moon shape onto the wrong side of the yellow print fabric. Fuse the star shapes to the wrong sides of the assorted white prints, following the manufacturer's instructions. Cut out the shapes on th traced lines. Remove the paper backing from each shape.

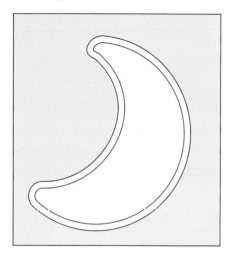

4. Referring to the appliqué placement diagram, position the moon and stars onto the gray print. Fuse in place, following manufacturer's instructions.

5. Using your favorite appliqué stitch, sew the moon and stars onto the gray print.

Finishing

1. Layer the backing, batting, and quilt top. Baste the layers together and hand- or machine-quilt as desired.

2. Sew the 2½"-wide binding strips together to make one continuous strip. Press the strip in half lengthwise, wrong sides together. Sew the binding to the front of the quilt, aligning the raw edges. Turn the binding over the edge to the back of the quilt and hand- or machine-stitch in place.

Appliqué placement diagram

Petting Zoo

By Choly Knight
Finished size: 40" x 40" (102 x 102cm)

This adorable and fuzzy quilt makes a great play mat that is cozy and plush to sit on, and it's also covered in appliquéd animals made from super-soft minky that are impossible not to touch. Your baby can have fun petting them until he or she gets older and can learn to name the animals and match up the pairs. It would also make a lovely wall hanging for baby's room. The simple checker design can be done in a number of colors, from sweet and understated to wild and bold.

Materials

- ⅓ yard cotton fabric in Color A
- ⅓ yard cotton fabric in Color B
- ⅓ yard cotton fabric in Color C
- ⅓ yard cotton fabric in Color D
- ⅓ yard cotton fabric in Color E
- 1¼ yards cotton fabric for borders
- 1¼ yards cotton fabric for backing
- 1⅓ yards cotton fabric for binding
- 44" x 44" batting

Appliqué fabrics:
- ¼ yard or 9" x 18" remnant gray minky
- ¼ yard or 9" x 18" remnant white minky
- ¼ yard or 9" x 18" remnant blue minky
- ¼ yard or 9" x 18" remnant purple or pink minky
- ¼ yard or 9" x 18" remnant green minky
- One fat quarter in cream cotton
- One fat quarter in black cotton
Thread to match appliqué fabrics
Fusible web
Template plastic and templates on pages 158–159

Quilt originally appeared in *Sew Baby*

Quilt top assembly diagram

Appliqué
character
assembly
diagrams

Cut the various rectangle and square pieces from the fabric according to the chart below:

Fabric color	Size to cut	Number to cut	Seam allowance
A	9½" x 9½"	4	¼"
B	9½" x 9½"	3	¼"
C	9½" x 9½"	3	¼"
D	9½" x 9½"	3	¼"
E	9½" x 9½"	3	¼"
Vertical border	2¼ " x 36"	2	¼"
Horizontal border	2¼" x 40"	2	¼"
Binding	3½" x 48"	4	½"

1. Appliqué the characters. Cut and apply fusible web to the appliqué fabric. Using the illustrations on page 144 arrange the appliqué pieces. Iron and sew the appliqué pieces to the corresponding quilt square.

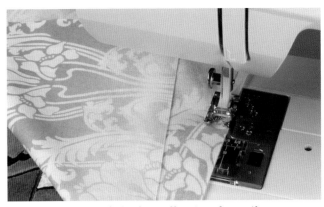

2. Sew the rows of blocks. Following the quilt top assembly diagram, create a row of Colors B, C, A, and D. Next, create a row of Colors D, A, E, and B. Then create a row of Colors E, B, C, and E. Lastly, make a row of Colors C, A, D, and A. Include the appliquéd blocks where indicated by the diagram.

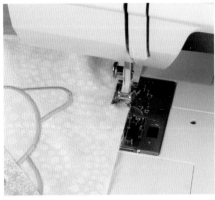

3. Sew the rows together. Sew the rows along their long sides, following the quilt layout illustration. This will create a complete four-block by four-block square.

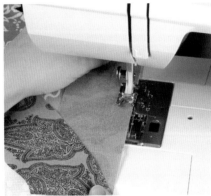

4. Sew the side borders. Sew the vertical border pieces to the sides of the quilt square.

5. Sew the top and bottom borders. Sew the horizontal border pieces to the top and bottom of the quilt.

6. Baste the quilt layers. Stack the backing fabric, quilt batting, and quilt top (in that order) on a large, flat surface. Smooth out as many wrinkles as possible and, working outward from the middle, begin pinning the layers together with safety pins every 5"–10".

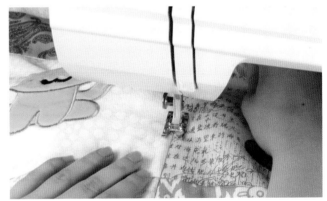

7. Quilt the layers. With a slightly longer straight stitch, sew through all the layers of the quilt along the edges of the blocks. Work from the center outward and smooth the fabric constantly, making sure all the layers are perfectly even. When it's complete, trim the excess quilt batting and backing sticking out from the quilt top.

8. Bind the quilt. Follow the binding instructions starting on page 58 or page 64.

Chocolate Mint Swirl

Made by Jean Ann Wright, quilted by Sue Bentley
Quilt size: 52" x 60"
Pineapple Block size: 8" x 8"

Dark brown and pastel solids combined with a fun polka dot give this quilt a flavor of colored candy with chocolate centers. The strips are placed so they create a swirl pattern, like chocolate gently stirred into a sweet, creamy mixture.

Materials

- Thirty 10" squares, or one layer cake
- 3 yards brown solid or brown "grunge" fabric
- 1¼ yard brown polka dot fabric
- 3¼ yards backing fabric
- Creative Grids® Pineapple Trim Tool (optional)

WOF = width of fabric

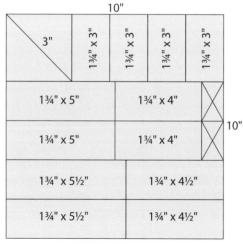

Cutting diagram

Cutting

Note: Follow the cutting diagram to cut the 10" squares for the blocks and border.

From each 10" square, cut:
- One 3" strip. From the strip, subcut:
  - One 3" square
  - Four 1¾" x 3" rectangles

Cut the 3" square in half diagonally to make:
- Two half-square triangles
- Four 1¾" strips. From the strips, subcut:
  - Two 1¾" x 5½" rectangles
  - Two 1¾" x 5" rectangles
  - Two 1¾" x 4½" rectangles
  - Two 1¾" x 4" rectangles

From the brown solid fabric, cut:
- Three 3" x WOF strips. From the strips, subcut:
  - Thirty 3" squares. Cut each square in half diagonally to make sixty half-square triangles
- Seven 2½" strips for binding

- Forty 1¾" x WOF strips. From the strips, subcut:
  - Sixty 1¾" x 5½" rectangles
  - Sixty 1¾" x 5" rectangles
  - Sixty 1¾" x 4½" rectangles
  - Sixty 1¾" x 4" rectangles
  - 120 1¾" x 3" rectangles

From the brown polka dot fabric, cut:
- Two 2½" x WOF strips. From the strips, subcut:
  - Thirty 2½" squares for block centers
- Six 6½" strips for borders Sew together end-to-end. From the long strips, subcut:
  - Two side borders 6½" x 48½"
  - Two top/bottom borders 6½" x 52½"

Quilt originally appeared in *Pineapple Play Quilts & Projects*

Making the Blocks

Note: To make a Pineapple block with a spiral design, you will add a strip of brown fabric to the strip of the same color in Round 2. Repeat for Rounds 3, 4, 5 and 6.

1. For Round 1, use four different colors of pastel strips. Sew a 1¾" x 3" pastel strip to opposite sides of a 2½" center square, right sides together. Press the seams toward the strips.

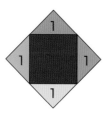

Round 1

2. In the same manner, sew a 1¾" x 3" pastel strip to the two remaining sides of the center square to complete Round 1. Press the block and trim Round 1 to size (using the Pineapple Trim Tool if desired).

3. Sew four 1¾" x 3½" brown solid strips to the block. Press and trim to complete Round 2.

Round 2

4. Sew two 1¾" x 4" brown solid strips and two different 1¾" x 4" pastel strips to the block in the same manner. Press toward the strips. Press and trim to complete Round 3.

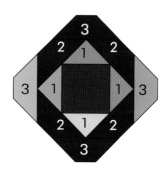

Round 3

5. Sew 1¾" x 4½" and 1¾" x 5" and 1¾" x 5½" strips to complete Rounds 4, 5, and 6, being careful to follow the color orientation of the block diagram to maintain the brown "swirl." Press and trim the block after each round is added.

6. Sew the pastel half-square triangles to the Round 6 brown strip and the brown half-square triangles to the Round 6 pastel strip to finish the block. Square the block to 8½" (using the Pineapple Trim Tool if desired). Make thirty blocks.

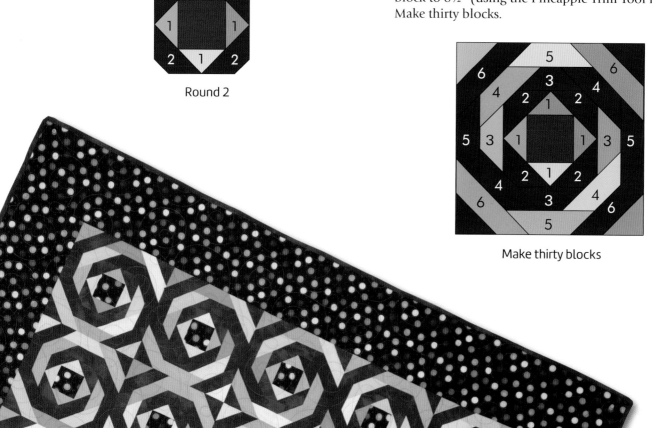

Make thirty blocks

Quilt Top Assembly

1. Arrange the blocks in six rows of five blocks each. The blocks are added with the pastel triangles in the upper left and lower right corners and the brown corner triangles in the upper right and lower left corners. Carefully watch the color orientation as you join the blocks into rows.

2. Sew the rows together to complete the quilt center. Press the seams.

Adding the Borders

1. Add the 6½" x 48½" side borders to opposite sides of the quilt center.

2. Sew the top/bottom borders to the quilt center. Press the seams.

Finishing

1. Layer the quilt top, batting, and backing. Baste the layers together and quilt as desired.

2. Sew seven 2¼" x WOF strips together end-to-end to make one continuous strip. Press the seams open. Press the strip in half lengthwise, wrong sides together, and sew to the raw edge of the quilt top. Fold the binding over the raw edges and stitch in place.

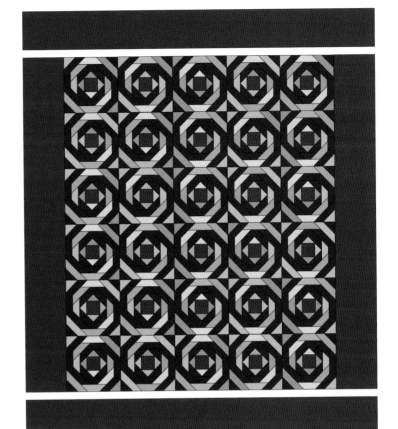

Quilt top assembly diagram

Templates

Baby Quilt templates

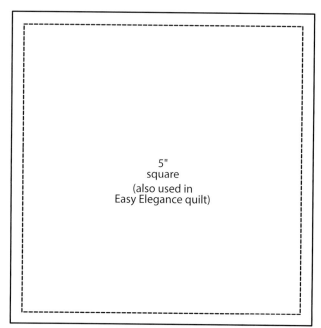

5"
square
(also used in
Easy Elegance quilt)

GO! die #55010
Square 5" (4½" finished) ; includes seam allowance
Enlarge 200%

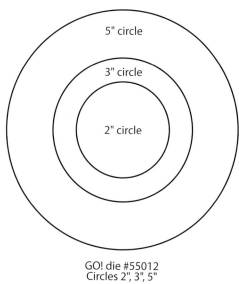

5" circle

3" circle

2" circle

GO! die #55012
Circles 2", 3", 5"
Enlarge 200%

Springtime for Baby template

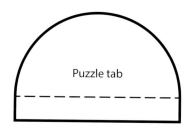

Puzzle tab

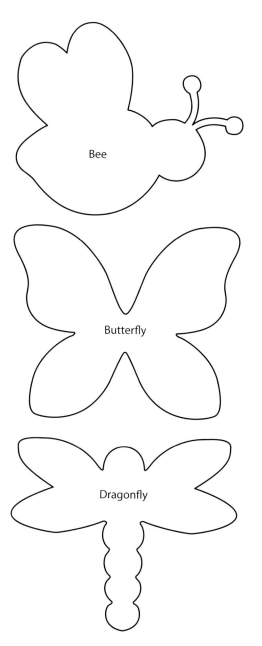

Bee

Butterfly

Dragonfly

GO! die #55030
Critters (bee, butterfly, dragonfly
Enlarge 200%

GO! die #55035
Alpha Baby
Enlarge 200%

4" heart

3" heart

2" heart

GO! die #55029
Hearts 2", 3", 5"
Enlarge 200%

Duck

Bear

GO! die #55037
Baby, Baby (duck and bear)
Enlarge 200%

GO! die #55331
Stems & Leaves
Enlarge 200%

Plaid Quilt/Argyle Quilt templates

Enlarge templates 500% for actual size.

Friends and Flowers templates

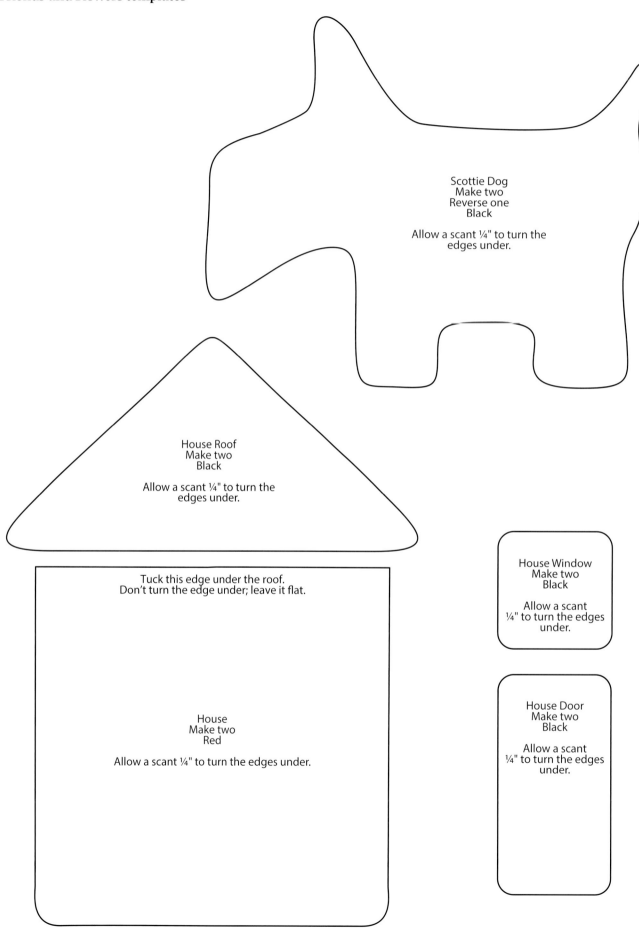

Scottie Dog
Make two
Reverse one
Black

Allow a scant ¼" to turn the edges under.

House Roof
Make two
Black

Allow a scant ¼" to turn the edges under.

House Window
Make two
Black

Allow a scant ¼" to turn the edges under.

Tuck this edge under the roof.
Don't turn the edge under; leave it flat.

House
Make two
Red

Allow a scant ¼" to turn the edges under.

House Door
Make two
Black

Allow a scant ¼" to turn the edges under.

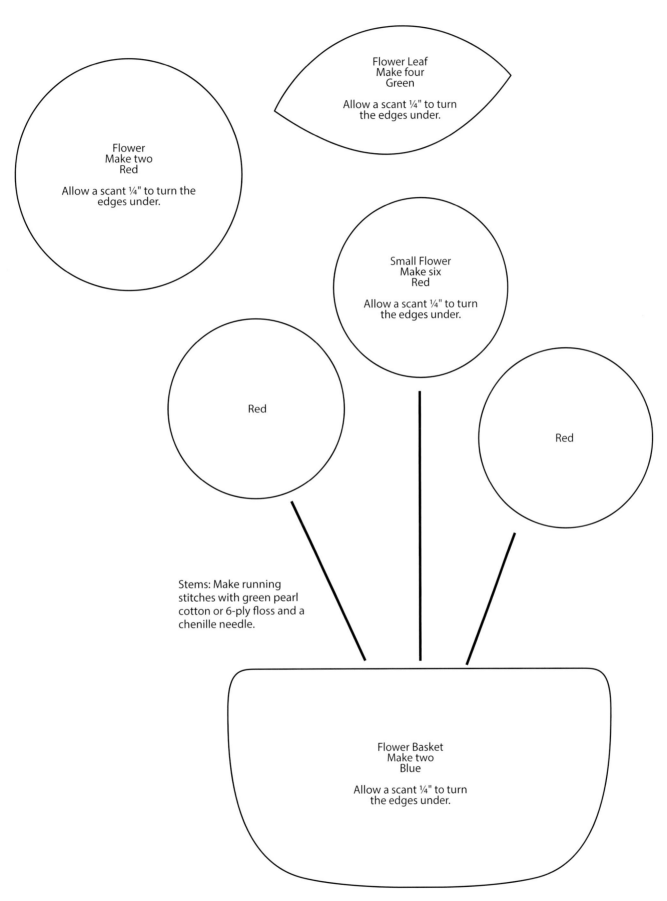

Flower Leaf
Make four
Green

Allow a scant ¼" to turn
the edges under.

Flower
Make two
Red

Allow a scant ¼" to turn the
edges under.

Small Flower
Make six
Red

Allow a scant ¼" to turn
the edges under.

Red

Red

Stems: Make running
stitches with green pearl
cotton or 6-ply floss and a
chenille needle.

Flower Basket
Make two
Blue

Allow a scant ¼" to turn
the edges under.

Note: Do not use buttons on quilts intended
for babies and young children.

Eye Spy Quilt templates

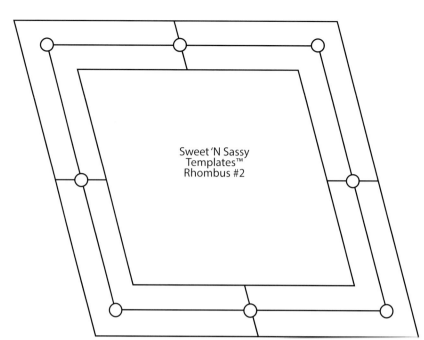

Sweet 'N Sassy
Templates™
Rhombus #2

Moon and Stars templates

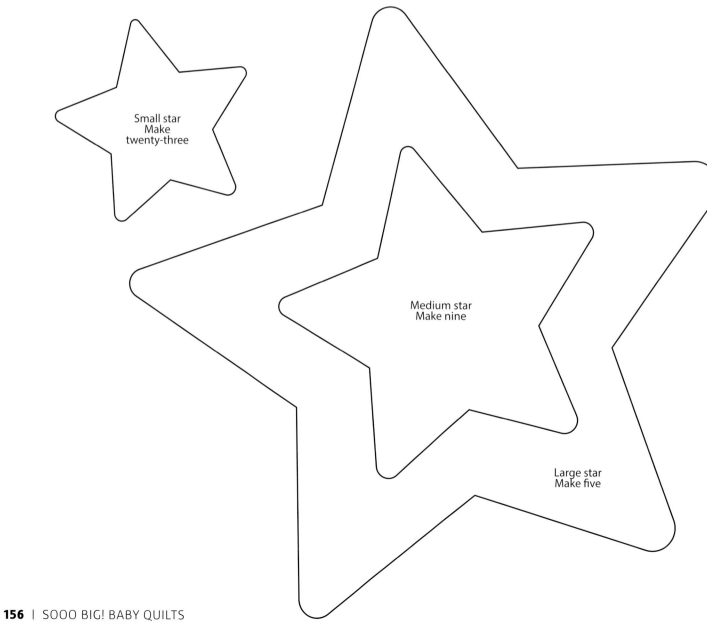

Small star
Make
twenty-three

Medium star
Make nine

Large star
Make five

Moon and Stars templates continued

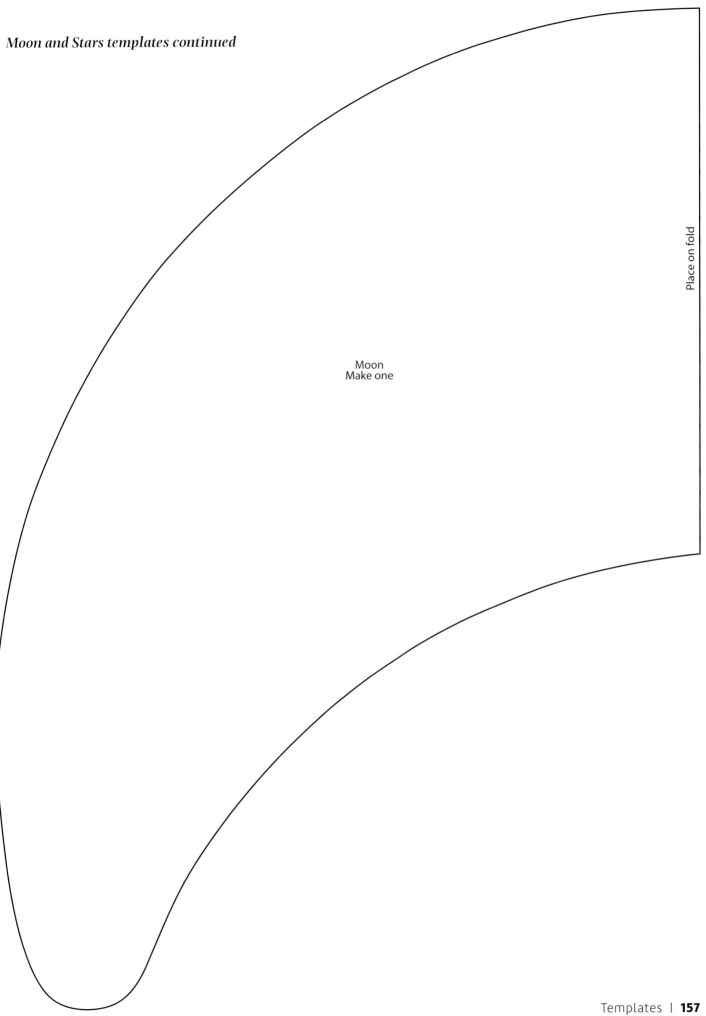

Place on fold

Moon
Make one

Petting Zoo templates

Enlarge templates 125% for actual size.

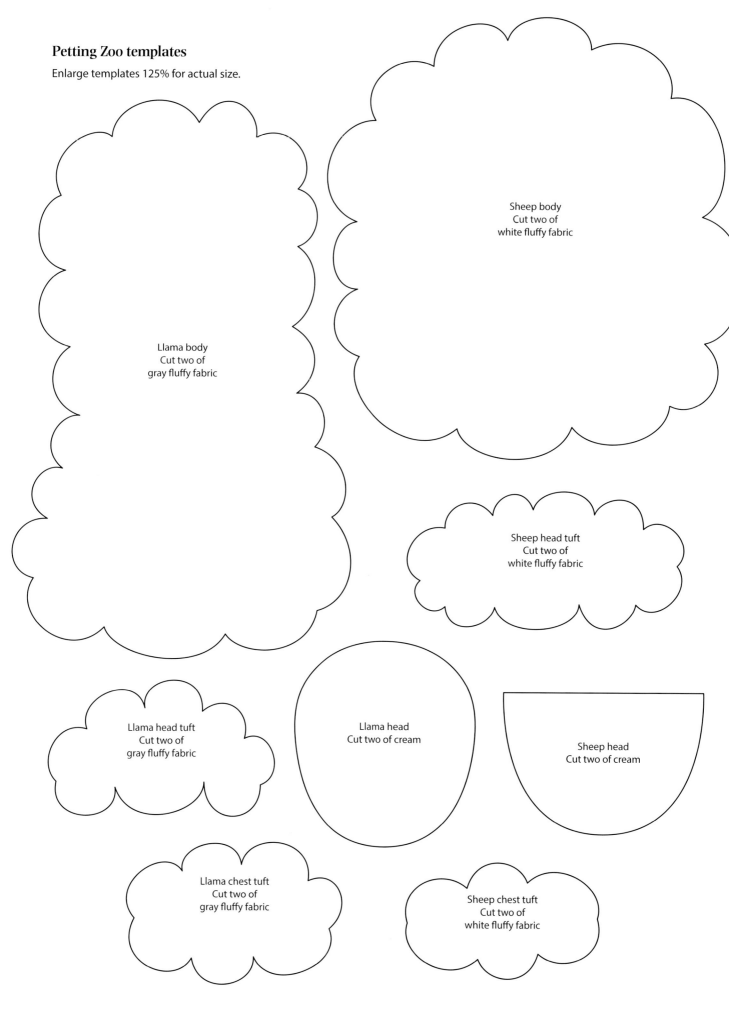

Sheep body
Cut two of
white fluffy fabric

Llama body
Cut two of
gray fluffy fabric

Sheep head tuft
Cut two of
white fluffy fabric

Llama head tuft
Cut two of
gray fluffy fabric

Llama head
Cut two of cream

Sheep head
Cut two of cream

Llama chest tuft
Cut two of
gray fluffy fabric

Sheep chest tuft
Cut two of
white fluffy fabric

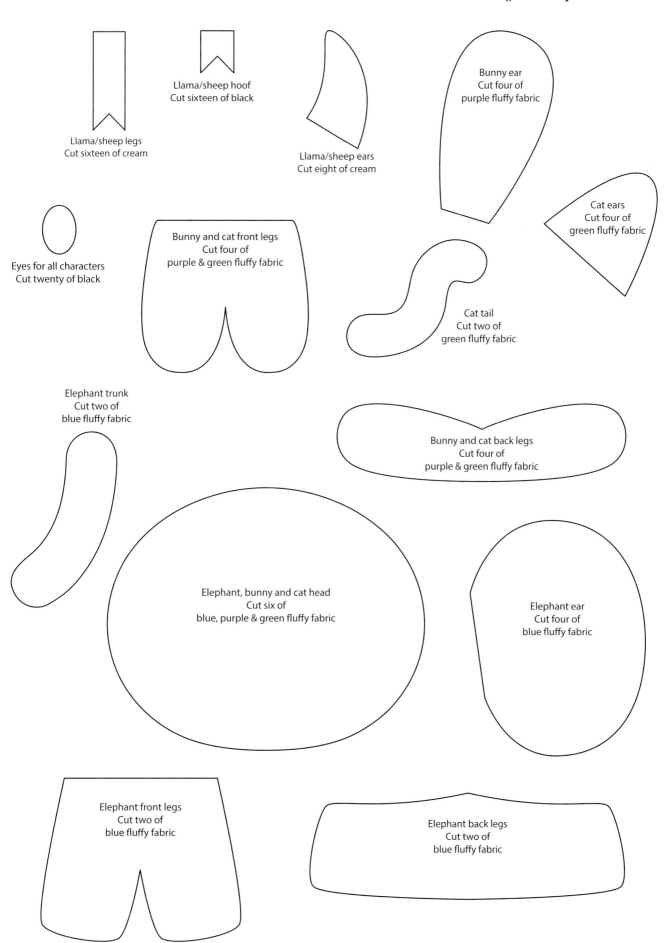

Llama/sheep legs
Cut sixteen of cream

Llama/sheep hoof
Cut sixteen of black

Llama/sheep ears
Cut eight of cream

Bunny ear
Cut four of
purple fluffy fabric

Cat ears
Cut four of
green fluffy fabric

Eyes for all characters
Cut twenty of black

Bunny and cat front legs
Cut four of
purple & green fluffy fabric

Cat tail
Cut two of
green fluffy fabric

Elephant trunk
Cut two of
blue fluffy fabric

Bunny and cat back legs
Cut four of
purple & green fluffy fabric

Elephant, bunny and cat head
Cut six of
blue, purple & green fluffy fabric

Elephant ear
Cut four of
blue fluffy fabric

Elephant front legs
Cut two of
blue fluffy fabric

Elephant back legs
Cut two of
blue fluffy fabric

Index

Photo Credits

J. Horn: 43
Matthew McClure: 54, 56–59, 60–65, 75, 78, 142–143, 145
Sue Voegtlin: 20, 24, 26–27, 29, 66–67, 83–84, 86, 88, 91, 98, 108–109, 118–119, 124–125, 128–129, 133, 146–148